Some of Satan's Major Lies Seen as Truth

To those who seek and follow the Way, the Truth and the Life

Fred DeRuvo

Copyright © 2009 by Study • Grow • Know

All rights reserved. Written permission must be secured from the publisher to use or reproduce any part of this book, except brief quotations in critical reviews or articles.

Published in Scotts Valley, California, by Study • Grow • Know
www.studygrowknow.com • www.rightly-dividing.com

Scripture quotations are from The Holy Bible, English Standard Version®, copyright © 2001 by Crossway Bibles, a publishing ministry of Good News Publishers. Used by permission. All rights reserved.

Images used in this publication (unless otherwise noted) are from clipartconnection.com and used with permission, ©2007 JUPITERIMAGES, and its licensors. All rights reserved.

All Woodcuts used herein are in the Public Domain and free of copyright.

All Figure illustrations used in this book were created by the author and protected under copyright laws, © 2009.

Library of Congress Cataloging-in-Publication Data

DeRuvo, Fred, 1957 –

ISBN 1448601401
EAN-13 9781448601400

1. Religion – Biblical Theology – Apologetics

Foreword

We know from many passages in Scripture that Satan is a liar. Christ said that lying is Satan's natural and normal language (cf. John 8:44). We think we know his lies, but interestingly enough, some of his best lies are the ones which cause many to balk at the basic doctrines of the Christian Faith.

Most of us want to know the truth. However, it is unfortunately defined differently by different people. Because of this, there is no real agreement and that gives rise to all sorts of truisms and standards that are nothing more than subjective.

This book is not a discourse on theological or doctrinal subjects with which the average Christian should already be aware. It is assumed that each Christian is able to know what they believe and why they believe it. Areas concerning salvation, the deity of Christ, the Trinity and others have been fought over and dealt with by many individuals over the centuries. Christians have no excuse not to know those things, especially with the many books that have been written on these subjects, besides the Bible itself.

This book is meant to open the eyes to some of Satan's more modern-day lies; the ones he is using now, which not only vilify the Christian as far as the world is concerned, but wind up pitting Christian against Christian. It is important to keep in mind that the true Church is filled with tares (professing Christians, but not truly Christian). We *may* be able to discern who they are, but probably not. Because of that, it is becoming increasingly important to be aware of Satan's lying schemes.

In this day and age, when the truth seems to be up for grabs, learning what the world is doing and preparing for, can wind up shedding a great deal of light on things. Knowing and understanding his methods and lies serves to fit the Christian with another weapon in the fight to seek and save the lost, and to live our lives for God's glory.

- Fred DeRuvo - September, 2009

Contents

Chapter 1: When Truth is a Lie 7
Chapter 2: No Room for Hatemongers 14
Chapter 3 New Age Divinity 33
Chapter 4 All Roads Lead to Rome 46
Chapter 5: The Great Evacuation 62
Chapter 6: Green! Green! Let's Go Green! 89
Chapter 7: Hell is So Passé 98
Chapter 8: The Days of Noah…Again 126
Notes and Resources for Your Library 156

ILLUSTRATIONS:
Rapture According to Satan 81
The Rapture and the Second Coming 85
15 Contrasting Events of the Second Coming 85
Promise, Program and Timing of the Rapture 87
It is All for His Glory 104
As It Was in the Days of Noah 150

Chapter 1

When Truth Is a Lie

"Unsinkable"

It would be safe to say that most of us recognize the importance of *truth*. To have more than one truth not only muddies the water, but makes it impossible to establish much of anything.

There can only be one true direction called north, another, we call south, another labeled East and yet another we affirm as being west. We cannot assume that it is fine for us to refer to a direction one way, while others refer to that same direction in another way.

The same is true in just about everything, whether it is math, physical sciences, driving, and a host of other areas. Truth is what puts all of us on the same plane, as it were, and without it, we might as well give up.

Relativity

Unfortunately, the one area that relies on truth the most, is fast becoming the one where the truth seems to become more and more *relative*. This is not a problem of today's society only. It existed during Christ's day and in fact, when Christ stood before Pilate during one of His illegal trials, Pilate straight out asked Jesus if he was, in fact, a king (cf. John 18:37a). To this, Jesus responded, *"You say correctly that I am a king For this I have been born, and for this I have come into the world, to testify to the truth Everyone who is of the truth hears My voice,"* (John 18:37b). Pilate, ignoring Christ's testimony regarding His own kingship, sardonically retorted *"What is truth?"* Apparently, he was not expecting, nor wanting an answer because the text tells us *"And when he had said this, he went out again to the Jews and said to them, 'I find no guilt in Him',"* (John 18:38).

The seeming relativity of truth (as far as the world is concerned) has been with us for ages and in fact, it was the very thing that created the trap which caused Adam and Eve to turn against God. Satan had cleverly come along and planted doubt in their minds, and he did so by attempting to establish a lie as if it was a fact.

In Genesis 3, we read the words that stated in effect that God was a liar, *"The serpent said to the woman, 'You surely will not die!'"* (Genesis 3:4). He immediately followed that up with *"For God knows that in the day you eat from it your eyes will be opened, and you will be like God, knowing good and evil,"* (Genesis 3:5). This is all that he said, but it was enough to push Adam and Eve into the realm of sin through unbelief (in God's Word) with the outward manifestation of actually eating the forbidden fruit.

Satan's Two Purposes

Satan is a liar and according to one writer, he has always had two purposes in mind that he wants desperately to achieve and lying is his chief means of getting there. *"The two great activities of Satan...are referred to in 2 Thessalonians 2:4, in connection with the Man of Sin, who will be Satan's last and greatest manifestation. This being is spoken of as he ' who opposeth and exalteth himself above all that is worshipped.' These two activities are inseparable in that, while Satan is seeking to exalt himself above all that is called God or that is worshiped, he can keep his subjects or prolong his own existence only by an unceasing warfare in which he opposes himself against God. Whether Satan believes he may yet succeed in spite of the decree of the cross and the evident superior power of God, is not revealed."*[1]

Of course one of the best ways he can accomplish this is by creating lies that *seem* to be truthful, but are anything but truthful. This is exactly what is happening today, not just in the world, but in Christian circles. More and more professing Christians espouse the viewpoints that will be highlighted in this book. It is largely because they do not know how to study the Bible, they would prefer not to take the time to study the Bible, and they wrongly believe that by listening to a pastor's message once a week (or so), they have learned something. Maybe they have, but that would be like eating only once per week. It would not take too long before a person died of starvation.

Because we do not actually suffer from persecution as many did before us, Christians today have become incredibly lukewarm and comfortable with their position in life. While the economy may go up and down, and while jobs may come and go, it will all work out in the end, we say. God will take care of us. The problem with that of course, is that God has not left us here (after we become Christians) so that we can be fed and satisfied with this life. He has left us here for *His* purposes. It is actually important to study His Word, to know what His overall plan is and to understand that His plans include using *you* to bring others to a saving knowledge of Him.

John MacArthur put it bluntly recently when he said "*Now is not the time to make friends with the world. It is certainly no time to capitulate to worldly cries for pluralism and inclusivism.*"

What Is Your Temperature?

Without doubt, Dr. MacArthur is correct. No time is a good time for Christians to compromise the truth by attempting to be friends with the world. It all begins and ends with whether or not the Christian feels the need to make friends with the world. Unfortunately, Christians are not only incredibly lukewarm, but many also suffer from an impotence that is directly related to a lack of concern about *God's* plans and purposes. This lack of concern regarding God's plans and purposes is pushed out by a deep concern about what the world thinks of the Christian. We do not want to seem out of step. We do not want to be viewed as painfully old fashioned. We desire to be in step with the modern world, and it is because of this that many of the things of God fall by the wayside.

For instance, it has become faddish to speak of being "green" when it comes to the environment. We must eliminate waste at all costs. We must bring pollution down to zero particulate matter spewed into the atmosphere above us. Beyond this, we must recycle everything possible. To be sure, these are good things to do, but it is also amazing that while we are involved in being "green," we seem to have forgotten that God wants us to be *evangelists* for Him and His gospel mission to take out for Himself a people from all nations (cf. Matthew 28:20)!

So Satan lies and he lies very well. He is not someone who should be taken for granted. His power and ability should certainly be at the least respected, as one would respect any type of poisonous snake, which has the power to kill. Only uninformed or naïve individuals would attempt to go near, or pick up a rattlesnake without thought of potential harm, or even death. The potentially fatal clout within the rattlesnake's venom speaks for itself, and most are simply incapable of fighting off the effects of its poison, without medical intervention.

It is the same way with Satan. We need to understand that he is constantly working to set up his own system whereby he will be proclaimed as THE one and only god. That is his program and has always been his program. For Christians to think that he takes his program lightly is foolhardy on our part. We cannot underestimate his ability.

God's Grace and Strength Needed
At the same time, knowing that he is powerful at lying and deceiving should cause us to throw ourselves that much more fully on God's Word because it is the only anti-venom for his lies and treachery. The more we know of God and His purposes, the greater our relationship with Him becomes. As this occurs, our fight against the enemy of our souls takes on new meaning. While we learn with greater clarity that Satan has been defeated, we come to rely more and more on the fact that it is God, who has defeated him, not us. Since that is the case, relying on God should be automatic, yet not only is this not the case, but all too often, Christians cannot even verbally explain *what* they believe and/or *why* they believe it!

It is because of all of this that Satan, in essence, has what appears to be his way with us. We are hopefully aware of his schemes as we are supposed to be and certainly as Paul was (cf. 2 Corinthians 2:12), yet it is obvious that many are not. This is more than tragic. It is simply not right, and it dishonors God.

As long as Christians are unaware of the truth of God's Word, we are powerless to fight the onslaught of the enemy. We are quickly taken in, undone by his lying campaigns. Our mouths become closed and we have no retort.

Such was certainly not the case with Christ. After He was led out into the wilderness by the Holy Spirit, He was subjected to Satan's powerful temptations. In each case, Jesus responded with Scripture. In each case, Satan's schemes unfolded and the truth of Scripture penetrated his embattlements like a soldier breaking easily through the last line of defense. The reader is encouraged to read this incident, which is found in each of the first three gospels; Matthew 4:1-11, Mark 1:12-13, and Luke 4:1-13. Please pay special attention to the fact that Jesus did not waste time arguing with Satan. He simply responded to each temptation with God's Word. If this is what Jesus did, how much more do we need to do this?

And so for this reason, this book has been written. Certainly, not every lie of Satan is included here, but some of the more major lies that have become very prevalent in society today. Each lie is detailed and then we will see and discuss God's response to it. Without God and His Word, the Christian is nothing, unable to defend against the penetrating effects of our primary enemy. With God and His Word, the enemy stands defeated.

As in any fight, energy is expended and work must be done to maintain ground and recover any ground that is lost. The work that the Christian needs to be involved in is threefold:

1. Reading and knowing Scripture
2. Prayer leading to maturity in Christ, by submitting to Him, and His will
3. A humble willingness to follow Christ regardless of the cost

Against these things, Satan cannot for long stand. While we should never underestimate his power and ability, he is helpless against the Christian, who holds tightly to God's Word, in faith believing that what God promises, He will accomplish. The true nature of Satan's defeat is seen for what it is; actual, yet not actually realized.

Overemphasizing God's Love
The most interesting thing to this author regarding the lies of Satan presented herein, is the fact that all of them have one thing in common: *a complete misunderstanding of God's love.* To the people who adhere to one or more of the heretical beliefs highlighted herein, it becomes clear that they are heretical largely because of their overemphasis of God's love, to the exclusion of His other attributes, such as holiness and justice. This love is to them a gooey, soft-centered feel-

ing of emotion in which God is constantly reaching out to people, only wanting the best for them. While this is absolutely true, the flip side of is rarely discussed. His love is such they believe that He is even willing to overlook all manner of sin as if within His character, there is nothing even remotely resembling holiness, or justice. As much as God loves people, He hates sin on an equal level.

God is seen as someone who feels so *sad* for humanity, that all He wants to do is find some way to make us *feel better* about ourselves as we are now. He does not want us to change. He wants us to be comfortable in our skin, since He made us this way. This view of course, in no way considers sin at all as the vilifying factor in our separation from God. Beyond that, it gives no credence to the fact that man is responsible for that sin.

There will come a day of course when we will no longer have to deal with the problem of sin, either within ourselves or in others. We will also not have to consider again that there is someone who hates us so much that he is only stopped by the power of God's restraining hand.

For now though, this is the Christian life; living here on this planet until such a time as God calls us home. While we live here, the striving to live *for* Christ, and the enemy's assault against us will never cease. Glory to God though that we have Him within us, and His Word to guide and guard us. We are so foolish if we do not take advantage of those resources. Is there anything greater?

---

[1] Lewis Sperry Chafer, *Satan, His Motives and Methods* (Grand Rapids: Kregel 1990), 69

Chapter 2

No Room for Hatemongers

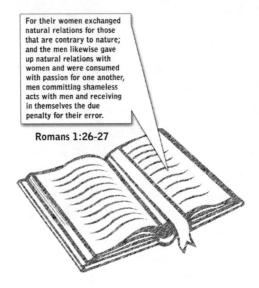

T he reader might be taken a bit back by the title of this chapter. What exactly does it mean? Put simply, it means that what used to be spoken of in whispers, and behind closed doors, is now being broadcast openly, accepted as *normal*. Those who oppose this new liberalism are immediately labeled with the one word that is meant to silence them: *hatemonger* or *hater*.

Not long ago, during the campaign of Proposition 8 which was held here in California, things heated up as they usually do when people's heart-felt beliefs are laid on the line. It was during this campaign when the Gay lifestyle was virtually foisted upon the average citizen from every direction.

In Your Face News

It was impossible to pick up a newspaper without being bombarded with in-your-face style articles. It was next to impossible to go one or two pages without reading about or seeing pictures of (or both) homosexual couples going about their daily lives. We saw pictures of two women who were in tears over the possibility that they would never have the choice to marry. There were pictures of men couples who for all intents and purposes seemed to do everything as heterosexual couples do. There were also photos of same-sex couples, but it was very obvious that one had adopted the *male* personality, while the other individual had adopted the *female* persona. For now, these people were living together as many do because of the lack of ability to be legally married.

The reader would either be forced to read through many of these articles, or wind up skipping over many pages of the newspaper to get to something that appeared interesting enough to read. It was not merely an article here or an article there. The front page of the paper on a near daily level, with many adjoining articles on the inside, announced their presence with headlines that were meant to attack as well as intimidate those who were against same-sex marriage.

I preferred not to get directly involved with those who wound up simply yelling at one another and decided to save my energy for the voting booth. The day of the election came and went and Proposition 8 passed, as it had the first time. Unfortunately, the first time it was overturned by a majority of California State Supreme Court Justices, so the only thing left was to modify the proposition and get it on the next ballot election.

As I write this, Proposition 8, having passed by a majority vote in the general election, has been *upheld* as legal by these same justices, with only one of them voting against it. So far, it remains the law, so those who did not become married are not able to get married in California, at least for now. Those same-sex couples who did legally get married prior to the election, are still married as far as the state is concerned. The Gay community has indicated though that they will not stop until Proposition 8 is overturned completely, allowing them to exercise what they believe to be their full spectrum of civil rights.

Sore Losers

Because of this situation, the vitriol, angst, and even hatred and animosity are palpable in some circles. It has become common place for militant homosexuals to disrupt meetings in churches, threaten to boycott, and in general, create a nuisance of themselves because they did not get what they wanted.

It was shortly after the Proposition 8 had been again passed by a majority that I visited an Internet forum dealing with this issue. I rarely take the time to do that anymore because I learned a long while ago that these types of conversations were normally counter-productive; all too often denigrating into nothing more than name-calling diatribes. The conversations were often controlled by people who either got their kicks by *instigating* problems, or the moderators themselves were for the "other" side, which in this case, means in favor of the homosexual community. That made it difficult to inject dialogue into the conversation that was in opposition to same-sex marriage, and expect to be treated fairly.

Of course the other problem with Internet forums is that most if not all people use a screen name; a nickname which hides their actual identity. This is a wise move, and I do the same thing. However, it is because of this that people feel free to really let loose on others. After all, they are safe enough because no one knows who they really are in daily life.

In following a bit of the conversation, it was interesting to me how little people knew about AIDS and in general how they were willing to attack those who viewed life differently than they did. Most people have probably forgotten that the disease known as AIDS, was originally named the Gay-related immune deficiency (GRID).[1] This was in 1982 when the disease first became known. Of course, many gay groups became instantly upset with that, because it drew attention to them and their lifestyle. The name was quickly changed to AIDS, which stands for Acquired Immune Deficiency Syndrome. This was much more of a generic name that did not draw attention to just gays. It included drug users who shared needles and also those who were sexually promiscuous. The problem though is that it is a known fact that AIDS has its roots in Africa and somehow made it to the United States. It first established itself within the gay community among men.

After a while, there were certainly enough people who were having sexual intercourse with others so that those who were bi-sexual (and had unknowingly had sexual intercourse with a gay person who also had AIDS), transferred the AIDS disease to heterosexuals. The entire AIDS disease became an epidemic because of it. Just think, if people remained faithful to one sexual partner in marriage only, would the world have this problem?

Yet, the Gay community does not want to take responsibility for the spread of AIDS. They would prefer that the world believe that the disease is just as common among gays as among heterosexuals. Of course, that cannot now be denied due to how widespread it has become, and the speed with which it has done so.

At any rate, when I brought some of this information to the fore and posted it on this forum, I was immediately attacked. I could almost hear one person in tears as she wrote something like "Oh no! AIDS is a disease of the blood! It's not a gay disease!" She's half correct. It is a disease of the blood, and while it is not *just* a gay disease anymore, it *began* as one. That was the point I was trying to make. No one on that forum could "hear" me though, because to them, I was a "hater" or "hatemonger." I had deigned to introduce *facts* into the conversation, instead of simply sympathizing with the plight of the same-sex two-some who could not enjoy all of what they believed are their civil rights.

There were a few individuals who said they were Christians, but when it came time to stating what God stated about it, their response was something like "God loves everyone." Okay, if they say so, but that is begging the question. The truth is that they did not want to say that homosexuality is wrong.

I decided again (against my better judgment) to offer my two cents, which I did. Essentially, it was along the lines of "Homosexuality is wrong. It goes against societal norms, but more importantly it is wrong because God says it's wrong." As you can imagine, that did not go over any better with most people than my previous comments.

Immediately, two people began bombarding anything I posted with terse rejoinders such as "Take your hate and go somewhere else!" or words to that effect. Immediately, the problem became *me,* so my efforts turned into attempting to explain that I was *not* filled with hate toward anyone. It did not matter though. They had latched onto what they felt was a good thing, and they were willing to wield it like a proverbial club, beating me over the head with it until I apparently yelled "Uncle!"

Just the Facts, Ma'am
I did not yell anything actually. I simply continued to post here and there, fully realizing that my posts were not going to make any difference. I tried a number of avenues like "If I say prostitution is wrong, I'm not directing hatred toward the prostitute. If I say that lying is wrong, I do not hate the liar. If I say that stealing is wrong, I am not spewing animosity toward the thief. In the same way, if I say that ho-

mosexuality is wrong, there is not one iota of hateful sentiment in that statement."

That of course did not matter either, and I knew it would not matter. The only reason I said it was because it needed to be said, and because I was certainly not going to leave with my tail tucked between my legs. Again, with immediacy, comments like "You're a hater!" and "Take your hate somewhere else!" filled the board, usually by the same few people. Of course one of the reasons they did this was to cause my posts to go lower and lower until they went to the next page where they would not be so easily seen. The other reason they did this was an attempt to make me cower, hoping to stop me from any further posting. They also hoped this was serve as a preemptory strike in case others had thoughts about agreeing with me.

The one Christian who had piped up before with "God loves everyone" *did* actually post something, but it was nothing that would darken the cloud over his head. His comment was "When you post, you should do what I do so that you do not offend people. Don't say homosexuality is wrong. Talk about how much God loves people." But you know, sin is sin and needs to be called that.

So while this individual made himself feel better because others immediately gave him an electronic pat on the back, the truth of the matter is that he was merely seeking the accolades of men. He apparently did not care whether or not homosexuality is wrong. What he *cared* about was what people thought of *him*. He certainly got in return what he played for by posting comments that would offend no one. However, by not officially taking a stand, he was seen as siding with those who were pushing for the overturn of Proposition 8. He was telling them that he was not going to stand in their way.

One of my last posts on that particular forum explained my position again, verifying that if someone says prostitution, or stealing, or lying, or driving without a license, or going over the speed limit, etc., are wrong, they are not making those statements out of angst, anger or hatred. They are merely repeating (in most cases), the law that oversees the actions of people in society. Since it is perfectly fine for someone to voice their opinion that prostitution is morally wrong (even where it is lawfully legal), that is their opinion, and they have a right to voice it.

I furthered wrote that when I make the statement that homosexuality is wrong, I say it the same way as I say these other statements. As soon as I make that statement about homosexuality though, I am seen as a "hater." This of course makes absolutely no sense, and it deprives me of my right of freedom of speech. It also impinges on my religious beliefs. However, more than that, the charge that I am a "hater" is an effort by the opponents of Proposition 8 to silence me. Even though most would see the hypocrisy in that label, when it is only used against those who speak out against homosexuality, it seems justified.

Immediately, as you might guess, I was referred to as a "hater," "hatemonger," and other things for making that post. It did not matter though. I had stayed long enough (two days) and left, having said what I wanted to say, and I said what was truth, according to the Scriptures.

Truth Not Wanted
The truth in this case of course is not what society deems to be the truth. The truth is what God deems to be the truth and in fact, that is *always* the case, or should be. Christians need to continually understand that difference. Failing to do so means compromising biblical principles for the world's and that never makes God happy.

One of the other very interesting things that have come out of this entire issue of same-sex marriages is that we now know for certain that the homosexual community will not give up their efforts to overturn what is believed by the majority to be a morally upheld law. The homosexual community has stated that they will never give up the fight.

They continue to boycott business who donated in favor of Proposition 8; some even going so far as to make threatening phone calls to the owners of these businesses. They continue to parade around cities decrying the alleged inhumanity of Proposition 8, and they continue to spew their vitriolic rhetoric *at those in favor of Proposition 8*. They do not even really care whether someone is listening or not. They simply want people to know that they exist and will show no signs of stopping their assault on what *they* believe to be an immoral law.

As long as they remain within the confines of the law (and at least *some* have opted to attempt to either circumvent the law, or break it altogether), with their efforts, then they are perfectly justified in trying to bring their opinion to fruition. However, if the shoe was on the other foot and Proposition 8 *had* been defeated, no amount of sarcasm, impatience and vitriol would be spared for those who took up the same type of battle cry to overturn Proposition 8's defeat!

The Shoe on the Other Foot
There would be no patience shown for those of us who would do the same thing the homosexual community is doing by working within legal system to again change the law so that same-sex marriage was not legal. We would be called every name in the book. We would be told we should give it up and go away because the legal system had spoken. Our businesses would be boycotted and harassing phone calls would be made. This type of attitude would be directed toward those us who, not satisfied with the outcome of the election, would continue to work within the system to do what was legally necessary to make a future change.

For now, because "they" have lost and "we" have won, "we" are viewed as being haters. So what has actually occurred is this: what has always been considered to be morally repugnant and wrong in society (by all except the extreme liberal edge), has now not only slowly been becoming more and more "right," but those who oppose it are now labeled "hatemongers."

Really though, when you consider it, what has actually changed? The only thing that has changed is the definition of what is *now* morally right. I and millions of others like me continue with the opinion that homosexual marriage is wrong and should not be made law. That has not changed. What has changed is how people *view* this same issue.

Of course, to make matters more difficult, you have the A-list celebrities speaking in favor or and giving their money to groups that support same-sex marriage. Their speeches involve comments like "these folks need to be able to exercise all of their civil rights," or "homosexuals would probably have a much lower rate of divorce than the Christian community" and other comments, to that effect.

However, in reality, these comments make no difference as far as God or His Word is concerned. If God states that something is wrong, then it is wrong because He is the One who decides. While I am certainly very aware of how those within the homosexual community attempt to distort the Scriptures so that they are able to state that God is not against homosexuality, the truth remains that they are distorting the clear teaching of God's Word.

Persecution Ramping Up
So in the end, what are we left with here? We are left with the fact that a type of persecution is ramping up against those who desire to uphold God's Word. People who are willing to risk being called "hatemonger," stand up to be counted when push comes to shove. They certainly are not worrying about being counted by the people of this world. They are concerned about being counted for *God*. That should be the Christian's concern.

While it is never good to speak an opinion in anger, it is always good to come out against something that is diametrically opposed to God's Word.

It is clear from Scripture that homosexuality is aberrant. All one has to do is search the Scriptures to find out that it was at one point considered to be an especially terrible sin (cf. Genesis 19:6-7, 24-28; 2 Peter 2:6). In Genesis 19, Lot was so nervous about what the men outside his door wanted to do to his two visitors (angels sent by God), that he offered his virginal daughters for these men to do what they wanted to do!

They Were Just Not Hospitable
I recall having a conversation with a person who considered himself to be a Christian, but was very liberal in his ideas about Christianity. We were discussing this very issue related to Sodom and Gomorrah. My friend stated that the sin of Sodom and Gomorrah was not homosexuality, but instead it was a (are you ready?)...*lack of hospitality.* So apparently, God destroyed these twin towns because they were not friendly enough! The sad part is that my friend actually believed this in spite of the wording of the text. Because the original Hebrew word employed in the text – *yada* – was used, it can connote knowing as in *getting to know someone,* or knowing as in *having sexual relations with someone.*

Of course the real difficulty with this position is that if the actual reason for Sodom's destruction had to do with a lack of hospitality, then the oneness must fall on God Himself for destroying two cities for this reason alone! It could then be reasonably asked, why didn't God destroy many *other* cities that were just as inhospitable?

However, Lot's reaction of determining to not allow the men of the city to do such a *wicked* act cannot possibly allude to the fact that they had not had the chance to be *hospitable* to these strangers! To even suggest that this is the reason is ridiculous on these two counts alone.

We nod, smile, laugh or smirk (depending which side you are on), when we recall Jerry Falwell's words to the effect that "God made Adam and Eve, not Adam and Steve." In point of fact, this is absolutely true and cannot be denied. It is very obvious that God had set a standard for humanity and that standard was one of a heterosexual nature, not homosexual.

Had God ordained homosexuality, certainly He would have done that right from the beginning. Beyond this, it is doubtful that He would have made this sin against His law, punishable by death.

In other areas of the Bible, homosexuality is seen as equally horrendous. In fact, under the Mosaic Legal system, homosexuality was punishable by death (cf. Leviticus 18:22 and 20:13). Certainly, this author is not advocating that type of punishment and under the Mosaic Law, this law *only* extended to those within the nation of Israel, not to surrounding nations. It is clear though that God was highly offended by this practice and undoubtedly is just as offended by it today, but grace continues to stay His judgment.

Of course, often people will be heard making comments to the effect that if you are going to follow *one* law of the Mosaic system, you have to follow *all* of them. In other words, why simply pick out homosexuality as being wrong? What about eating certain foods that were forbidden in Leviticus, as well? What about selling your children into slavery? There are many, many things that are forbidden in the book of Leviticus, so to simply choose to castigate homosexuality is unfair, we are told.

The problem with this view is a complete *lack* of understanding of Levitical ceremonial law and laws that came under the umbrella of the Mosaic system. Many were not directly related to the ceremonial laws; "*the prohibitions against homosexuality in Leviticus 18 and 20 appear alongside other sexual sins – adultery and incest, for example – which are forbidden in both the Old and New Testaments, completely apart from the Levitical codes. Scriptural references to these sexual practices, both before and after Leviticus, show God's displeasure with them whether or not any ceremony or idolatry is involved."*[2]

Proof of this can be seen in the New Testament, one of the favorite places people who support homosexuality point to for support. In a number of passages, Paul examines the type of person who he says, will not inherit the kingdom of God. He makes quite a list and among them are those who are homosexual (1 Corinthians 6:9-10). It can be argued (though not successfully) that in the original language, Paul does not use the word "homosexual." That is certainly true enough. However, he does use a few words to describe that lifestyle; *malakos*, which is translated *effeminate*. The meaning of this word according to Vine is *"not simply a male who practices (sic) forms of lewdness, but persons in general, who are guilty of addiction to sins of the flesh."*[3]

Wuest further clarifies the concept in his expanded translation of the New Testament, "...*men who are guilty of sexual intercourse with members of their own sex...*"[4] Paul again refers to this sin in 1 Timothy 1:10-11, where the word "sodomite" is used.

Probably, the most well known passage in the New Testament regarding homosexuality is found in the book of Romans 1:18-28. It is in this section of Scripture that Paul is explaining why there is not one person who is without excuse before God. All stand condemned and Paul provides the reasons why this is the case. In some sense, people get to a point where God finally gives them over to their most aberrant passions. He does this because these people wind up continually suppressing the truth (cf. Romans 1:18). They do everything they can to ignore God, not even consider Him while at the same time, being embroiled in deep sin.

Because God gives them over to their own passions, they sink lower and lower until finally they find themselves in *"degrading passions; for their women exchanged the natural function for that which is unnatur-*

al, and in the same way also the men abandoned the natural function of the woman and burned in their desire toward one another, men with men committing indecent acts and receiving in their own persons the due penalty of their error," (Romans 1:26-27). It is next to impossible to read this page and *not* know what Paul is talking about here. However, some within the homosexual community take this passage to mean that these people are sinning not because they are involved in homosexuality, but because their passions or lusts are left fully uncontrolled.

The homosexual misappropriates, denigrates and in general devalues the Word of God. Author Joe Dallas, himself once fully involved in the homosexual community, yet attended church, pulls back the curtain on how the biblical view of homosexuality is viewed by those who participate in that lifestyle.

Dallas states *"While showing a measure of respect to the Bible, gay Christians generally negate its authority or its sufficiency, or they claim it has been mistranslated, and thus misunderstood, in modern times."*[5]

Just Too Difficult To Translate
Beyond this, many leaders within the Gay movement state outright that the language of the Bible is too complex and even complicated for the average person to understand. They claim it takes a language expert to properly deal with passages concerning homosexuality. To this Dallas responds with, *"Oddly enough, this inability to understand the Bible seems to apply only to references to homosexuality. Read virtually any gay Christian material and you will find the generous use of other Scriptures, with nary a concern for their original Greek or Hebrew meaning. But on the subject of same-sex contact, gay Christians show a deep, sudden concern for historical, linguistic, or contextual accuracy."*

Many homosexuals within the gay Christian arena as well as the non-Christian arena, are quick to point to Jesus, who it is stated, said absolutely nothing about homosexuality, much less came out against it.

These folks, who lean on Jesus for support, do so by highlighting the fact that Jesus spoke of *loving people.* This of course, is merely an argument from silence. The absence of Jesus speaking about, or condemning the practice of homosexuality *implies* that it is not wrong.

This particular argument that many find useful, also presupposes that Matthew, Mark, Luke and John have more authority than any other portion of recorded Scripture. In fact, Paul or other writers will often be denigrated as being far less authoritative than Jesus Himself. After all, Jesus was/is God, therefore His Words by virtue of that fact, must have more authority. However, if it is true that the entire Bible is God's Word to humanity, then all of it carries equal weight.

It would be foolish to say that the tremendous doctrinal truths found in Romans or Hebrews for example, are not as weighty as anything Jesus said. It is clear that these books unearth far-reaching doctrinal truths that the gospels simply to not include. The largest reason for this is the fact that the gospels are presented as *narratives* of a Person's life; Jesus. In many ways, these four books present different aspects of Jesus, yet they all do so in a narrative style, suggesting a story.

All the other epistles of the New Testament (except for Acts), deal with doctrinal matters, or some area of biblical theology. The truths set forth in these epistles cannot, nor should not be understated. By no means should they be seen as less authoritative simply because Jesus Himself did not speak those words.

There are many things that Jesus did not speak about, but this does not give us license to take His silence as affirmation of something. Does Jesus specifically say anything about incest, for instance? How about child pornography? It would be ridiculous though to assume that because Jesus did not speak specifically about these things that He was in favor of them. We have already learned that Paul taught against homosexuality in a number of places. Though Jesus did not discuss it, His *silence* on the subject is seen by those within the homosexual community to trump Paul's words.

The Gay Agenda Clearly Seen
It is not at all difficult to discern what the gay agenda is for the world. Clearly, what is still seen as abnormal, will one day be seen as *normal.* This is the hope of the gay community. They wish to be treated as normal although they embrace something the God has declared abnormal.

Within the gay community many groups exist, which have their own particular niche, emphasizing one aspect or another of the homosexual community. One such group called GLAAD, has a presence on the Internet, and one of the things they do on their website is to keep track of programs (movies, TV shows), in which gay people are depicted positively. This assumes of course that gay people are not in and of themselves positive people, but the battle to ensure that gay characters are not shown in a bad light, continues.

It is becoming a very common practice for one celebrity after another to "come out" and express with openness their gayness. In fact, so many have done this that it becomes anti-climactic when one after another continues to pour out into the open, tripping over themselves to see who can get to the podium first in order to profess their appreciation for those within the homosexual community. The truth of the matter lies in the fact that most celebrities know that by *not* agreeing with the views of the homosexual community in Hollywood, they will have precious little film and/or TV work in Hollywood.

GLAAD has taken pains to include an area on their website called *TV Gayed: GLAAD's Weekly Guide to What's LGBT on TV*. This is the section where gay characters are kept track of each week. Having kept an eye on this aspect of their website for a bit, it is interesting to note that the instances of gay characters in Hollywood have grown a great deal over time.

However, it also appears that things are not going as well as could be hoped. On another page of their website called *Where Are We?*, GLAAD makes this statement *"the number of LGBT series regular characters found on scripted programming on mainstream cable networks has decreased from last year's analysis, from 40 to 32."*[6] This is in reference to gay characters on mainstream media programming, including daytime soap operas, talk shows, evening soaps and other TV programs.

Over all though, GLAAD does not seem to be too concerned, because they follow the above statement with *"The presence of LGBT-focused cable networks, HERE! and LOGO, which program, specifically for LGBT viewers, add additional representations. These two networks alone will provide 39 additional series regular LGBT characters, more than all the other cable networks combined."*[7]

As activists, GLAAD has stated, in no uncertain terms, that they are not giving up on mainstream TV programming. *"GLAAD will continue to work with the broadcast and cable networks to encourage more LGBT representations on television, and to make those representations fair, accurate and more diverse."*[8]

Of course it is not simply GLAAD that is doing what they feel they need to do to ensure a future for gay characters on TV and in movies. Other far more militant groups, such as Queer Nation will do what it takes to keep the issue of gay rights in front of the eyes of the nation, for however long it takes to bring their agenda to fruition. The people from this group are absolutely unafraid to confront people regarding their views on homosexuality; if they believe those views will curtain the rights of gay people.

Just today (as this was written), it was announced on the Internet that gay marriage became legal in New Hampshire. Governor John Lynch is quoted as saying, *"Today, we are standing up for the liberties of same-sex couples by making clear that they will receive the same rights,* *responsibilities — and respect — under New Hampshire law," Lynch said."*⁹

According to this same article, referencing the bill that was just passed it appears that churches will be able to decide whether or not they wish to be involved in gay weddings. *"Churches will be able to decide whether to conduct religious marriages for same-sex couples. Civil marriages would be available to both heterosexual and same-sex couples."*¹⁰

Christian: Stand Your Ground
So when all is said and done, what does the Christian do? We do not give in to these groups and change our opinion because they yell louder, or sound meaner, or act scarier through confrontation. Certainly, according to the United States Constitution, these groups and its members have every right to attempt to modify laws, as long as they work within the confines of the law to achieve their own desired end.

At the same time, Christians have a higher law and that law – God's law – supersedes any and every man-made law. Our first responsibility is to not shrink from what will likely become greater attacks on the Christian's point of view.

However, many who would call themselves Christian have a different agenda. Even those involved in cults like Mormonism have taken a second look. On the Internet is a website which is simply titled *Seeking Forgiveness*. On it are listed individual apologies by individual Mormons, who stand in opposition of their church's position, which came out against same-sex marriage. Apparently, the site dates back to November of 2008. As of this writing, there were 31 individual apologies listed.

Another pro-gay website plaintively speaks of the recent California Supreme Court's decision to upheld Proposition 8 with these words,

*"**Our worst fears have come to pass.** The California Supreme Court just ruled that a slim majority of voters could eliminate the right of same-sex couples to marry. This unjust decision flies in the face of our constitution's promise of equal protection."*

Same-Sex Marriage

Immediately underneath this statement is a set of links, one of which speaks of *"5 Ways to Win Marriage Back."* This involves pledging to speak with family and friends about having the freedom to marry, getting family and friends involved in the process to help to make this happen, volunteering to have in person conversations with those who may be in opposition to same-sex marriage, canvass the neighborhood with informational pamphlets about same-sex marriage and lastly, donate so that this pro-gay, pro-same-sex group will reach their goal of raising $500,000. This in turn will allow them to hire 25 organizers to "harness the grassroots energy."[11]

This group and others like them are doing whatever it takes to enable them to marry others of the same sex. Their campaign, *Win Back Marriage: Make It Real!* will undoubtedly not let up until they get what they feel entitled to have. So far, their site indicates that they have four individual groups, which are designed to *"support clergy and congregants from all faith traditions around the State of California to talk to their congregations about why the freedom to marry matters."*[12]

Christians Must Stand for God, Not the World

The Christian must confess the truth as taught in the Bible, and it must always be confessed with love, not remonstration, or condemnation. As far as the world is concerned, those who speak against homosexuality will continue to be viewed as "hatemongers" and probably worse. However, what the Christian needs to be concerned about is not what the world thinks of us, but what *God* thinks of us. It is to that end that we live and breathe.

[1] http://en.wikipedia.org/wiki/Gay-related_immune_deficiency
[2] Joe Dallas, *The Gay Gospel?* (Eugene: Harvest House Publishers 2007), 183
[3] W.E. Vine, *Expanded Vines*, (Minn. Bethany House Publishers 1984), 349
[4] Kenneth S. Wuest, *New Testament, An Expanded Translation* (Grand Rapids, Eerdmans 2004), 392
[5] Joe Dallas, *The Gay Gospel?* (Eugene: Harvest House Publishers 2007), 160
[6] http://www.glaad.org/whereweare, 06/04/2009
[7] Ibid
[8] Ibid
[9] http://www.msnbc.msn.com/id/31090983, 06/05/2009
[10] Ibid
[11] Ibid
[12] http://www.eqca.org/site/pp.asp?c=kuLRJ9MRKrH&b=5184355 06/06/2009

Chapter 3

New Age Divinity

In his book *Alien Encounter,* Chuck Missler explains how the New Age Movement began in the United States. It essentially stemmed from the writings of Helena Blavatsky, who lived in the middle to late 1800s, and whose writings gave rise to the Theosophical Society. Her many writings prompted other individuals like Alice Bailey and sci-fi writer H.G. Wells to pick up and carry her motif, if not her work, forward.

In essence, the New Age Movement is an actual religion; albeit one that defies certain definitions. People do not necessarily meet weekly in a house of worship, but they do have their own bible of sorts. One of the main books they look to is called *Oahspe: The Aquarian Gospel of*

Jesus the Christ; My Truth, the Lord Himself; and *My Peace, the Lord Himself;* this according to Missler.

The Commonality of Beliefs

What ties New Age adherents together is their beliefs. The one belief that they share is, as Missler points out, "the Source" or "the God of Force." Essentially, those within the New Age Movement believe that man is essentially divine. God already *resides* within everyone. The problem is that most of us are simply not aware of this fact. The New Age provides the knowledge, which help people *become* aware of their own inner divinity.

This is accomplished through the cycle of reincarnation. In each newly successive life, the adherent has another opportunity to become more and more aware of their own divinity (this is the hoped for scenario), until eventually no further reincarnations are required. The person will have at that point, come to full recognition of their own inner divinity and will have full control over their own life with the ability to create their own reality.

Should the person *not* make any headway with the new reincarnation, then they are actually moving backwards, and more reincarnations are necessary in order to achieve divinity. While it was extremely unusual to hear people talk of "past lives" a few decades ago, this is not the case today. It is common water cooler conversation; something accepted by many in today's world. Whether or not all who speak of reincarnation believe it, is something else entirely. However, it has become widely accepted to discuss it openly without fear of being ridiculed. In fact, because of the plurality of eastern cultures which have grown exponentially over the last twenty or thirty years, talk of and belief in reincarnation has become quite acceptable.

Often within the context of the New Age Movement, the phrase "Christ Consciousness" is used to define a particular *office* or *level of ascendency.* The Christ Consciousness then is *not* one particular individual, but something that all can (and should) achieve. So, in this regard, the Man Jesus was One who *became,* over His lifetime an Individual, who fully embraced the Christ Consciousness that was resident within Him. This, in effect, is what enabled Him to do all the things that He did while He lived on this earth, many of which appeared to be miraculous to us. This is the believed and expected norm for all people.

Christ is an Office, Not a Person

It was the office of the Christ Consciousness that provided Jesus with all of His ability. Apart from this, He was a human being, as all of us are human beings. Jesus then, worked diligently throughout His life to attain that level of ascendency. For the New Age person, this then is what they would call *salvation.* One works very hard, diligently trying to become *one with the universe*, in order to actualize the divinity that lies within. Once this level is achieved, the work is over and the person becomes an *ascended master*. In essence, then, those within the New Age movement and Maitreya himself deny that Jesus Christ actually came in the flesh (cf. 1 John 4:1-3). While Jesus the man was born on this planet and grew to understand the divinity within Him, He did not arrive on this planet *as God* from the start. This view, and all who hold it, is the view of the Antichrist.

Missler outlines the goals of the New Age Movement. *"They share the goal of creating a world peace through unification in a one-world spiritual system and a one-world government through a one-world leader of their choosing. Their covert goals are to abolish all systems based on the Bible by the year 2000, which is the beginning of the age of Aquarius. They endeavor to convert Western religious and philosophical belief systems into those of Eastern thought."*[1]

What this means of course, is that the way is being paved for a one-world government in which one individual could become supreme ruler, enforcing a one-world religion as well. Ultimately, this one-world religion will become the worship of him.

Sounds Like Science Fiction

It is certainly interesting to think about all the sci-fi movies, TV series and the like, which dealt with some maniacal, brilliant criminal whose goal is to take over the world. Most of the world views those programs as merely Hollywood's fascination with the science fiction genre. However, speak to anyone who has been an adherent of the New Age movement for any length of time, and while they might balk at the idea of a one-world ruler, they *do* look forward to a time of perpetual peace, which many believe will only occur *through* one individual.

What is easy for any true Christian to see, is that all of this leads to the climax of what Satan has wished for, worked for and believed he would gain, since he fell out of favor with God. He has always wanted to be like the Most High. It is this prideful arrogance that caused his fall from the high position he once held. In fact, of all the created beings, Satan as Lucifer was the highest and it is from that lofty height he fell, (cf. Isaiah 14:12-14; Ezekiel 28:12-20; Revelation 12:7-12).

Satan has never given up on his desire to not only be like the Most High, but to be worshipped as He is worshipped. Everything he has done in the past continues to do in the present and works toward in the future sees its culmination in this one goal. He longs to be worshipped as God is worshipped. He wants all of God's Creation to direct their gaze with adoring love and praise in his direction.

Daniel, Ezekiel and Revelation show us that he will have this, but for a short time, through the man he raises up of whom the Bible calls the Antichrist, the Man of Sin, the Man of Lawlessness, the Beast and other titles as well. It is fascinating that the New Age movement has become the primary vehicle for bringing this man out into the open. It is the New Age movement which is ushering in the day when the world will truly be one, under the barbaric leadership of this man. The Antichrist will be so filled with Satan, that in effect, when he finally sets himself up as God halfway through the Tribulation, people who worship him will be in fact worshipping Satan. Because he is rejected by the nation of Israel at that point, his terror will become fully unleashed and thus begins the Great Tribulation; the last three and a half years of man-led human history. This period of time will end with the physical return of Jesus Christ Himself.

Constance Cumby Weighs In

Constance Cumby has authored a number of books on the subject of the New Age. In many respects, she is considered an expert in the field of New Age. Her book *The Hidden Dangers of the Rainbow* begins with this ominous outlook:

"It is the contention of this writer that for the first time in history there is a viable movement – the New Age Movement – that truly meets all the scriptural requirements for the antichrist and the political movement that will bring him on the world scene.

"It is further the position of the writer that this most likely is the great apostasy or 'falling away' spoken of by the Apostle Paul and that the antichrist's appearance could be a very real event in our immediate future."[2]

Cumby wrote these words in 1983, and what she says certainly sounds ominous. Isn't the New Age movement merely made up of people who meditate and do Tai Chi, or something similar? Aren't they all merely harmless vegetarians? All evidence would seem to say no, but in fact the New Age movement is much more than this.

Cumby observes that within the New Age movement, the name of Maitreya is extremely important. It represents not a man, but a fifth reincarnation of Buddha; one who will take over the reins with his appearing to create a new world order. This in itself may be at least part of the reason there are believed to be *two* individuals referred to as Maitreya at this point in time; one that Cumby mentions and another who is often associated with Benjamin Crème. Interestingly enough, the Maitreya that Cumby highlights believes the Crème Maitreya to be an imposter and that Crème himself is inwardly a dragon.

Maitreya's Mission

Cumby indicates that *"Maitreya's followers are now in the last stage of the New Age scheme to take the world for Lucifer. Lucis Trust - formerly Lucifer Trust – ran ads in the* Reader's Digest, *which displayed The Great Invocation to Maitreya. The Great Invocation refers to The Plan. It says, ' Let Light and Love and Power restore the Plan on Earth'."*3

Cumby goes on to explain The Plan. It turns out to be nothing less than a Messiah for the new world he will establish, complete with new government along with a new, one-world religion.

Cumby also mentions one of the websites dedicated to Maitreya called Mission of Maitreya. Visiting the site introduces visitors to the teachings of Maitreya as well as statements like this: *"By entering this website, you are about to find the most amazing Truth. Humanity has been waiting for this Revelation for the last twelve thousand years."*4

The front page of this site continues by declaring that all major religions are really one in the same. *"In fact they are complementary and were sent to earth systematically by One God. When this is understood, the Path to Salvation (Eternal Divine Path) is known!"*5

The site unashamedly declares *"The Goal Of Life Is To Be(come) Divine, That Divinity (God) Is Everything."*6 This is the keynote address of the entire New Age movement. Perusing the site shows just how Christianity is viewed by these folks and by Maitreya himself.

As usual, with much of the information found on the site in the form of teaching, it is a mix of actual Bible Scripture, twisted to mean something other than what it actually means. While denying that he is the Antichrist, Maitreya claims that he is the last prophet of God to humanity. This is clearly stated in the Letter to Leaders posted on the website, with the title *God is Calling You (The Last Call)*, dated March

2, 2007. *"As Prophet Noah warned people in his time of the forthcoming flood, and Prophet Jonah warned the people of Nineveh of the coming disaster to their city, this is a warning from the Prophet of God (Maitreya) to humanity of the imminent disasters predicted to come at the end time!"*[7]

The letter continues, affirming that oneness of all major religions, *"There is no separation between religions, and there is only One God for the whole of humanity. Understanding how each of the world's religions have come in perfect order, and how each have an important part (Message) for mankind, is now revealed to man."*[8]

As is expected, Maitreya insists his lineage goes back not only to King David, but to Muhammad as well, and from this, he claims connection to the Hebrew race and the Lion of Judah. Maitreya has been here since 1977, and is waiting for the proper time to reveal himself to the world as the Messiah.

Go Figure

What is truly a66t67mazing is the fact that many of those within the church deny a number of aspects of biblical prophecy. Doctrines such as the literal Second Coming of Jesus, and a literal Antichrist who is to precede Him, are routinely rejected. Instead what is believed to occur is a *spiritual* return, in contrast to literal. The Antichrist is not a person, but an attitude. Some do believe in an actual Antichrist, but many of these also believe he has come and gone in the form of Nero, the infamous Roman Emperor. Many believe the return of Christ occurred in A.D. 70, with the destruction of Jerusalem and the Temple that was then standing. Of course this return of Christ is said to have been *spiritual* in nature, not physical. This is in spite of the testimony of the two angels in Acts 1, who informed the disciples (who had just seen Christ ascending into heaven), that this same Jesus would return in the same way they had seen Him go. It is natural and reasonable to believe that the angels meant that He would return *physically*. We are told in Revelation 1:7 that Jesus is going to return, and He will return on the clouds and *every eye shall see Him*. What else could this possibly mean than He will physically return and everyone will see Him because they will look up, and there He will be. With the advent of satellite, cable TV, the Internet and other media, it will be impossible to miss that event.

From the perspective of the New Age movement, they believe that one specific individual will appear to usher in the final age, which essentially becomes the new age. This new age, as has been stated includes a one-world government and a one-world religion, headed up by this one man, of whom the unsaved world will eventually worship.

Now of course the question must be asked, if the references to *the* Antichrist are not real, and any type of Tribulation/Great Tribulation is to occur, then why is Satan even bothering to teach these doctrines to New Age proponents? Satan appears to be working diligently to bring something about that has no basis in biblical fact, and will not occur (if conservative biblical scholarship is wrong). Why bother creating this entire façade if there is no chance of it occurring?

Satan Knows the Bible Better Than You
Satan knows the Bible, and he knows it better than anyone on this planet. He also has a much better vantage point to see what God is actually doing. Our vantage point requires a good deal of faith in many areas. Satan actually *sees* things in the making. He hears what is often being discussed. While he is unable to be everywhere at once and certainly does not know everything, he has a much better *actual* picture of what is happening throughout the world now. He is guiding much of it, with God's permission.

The point is that Satan knows what the Bible says what it teaches. He certainly understands the meaning of major prophetic utterances in Scripture, especially when they concern him. He knows that the Bible teaches the Rapture, and he is also well aware of the fact that Jesus is going to return to this planet. Jesus will return to judge and set up His kingdom, from which He will reign, seated on David's throne for 1,000 years. Since Satan knows this beyond doubt, it is obvious that he wishes nothing more than to stop that from occurring. He knows he is unable to stop the Rapture, so he has created this plausible story that the remaining people on earth will believe (for the most part). Those who do not believe it will probably not last too long, and may well keep quiet, though they themselves may finally become saved because of it. They will become one of those who evangelize the world, though it is clear from Revelation that the 144,000 who are sealed with God's seal will do the lion's share of that (cf. Revelation 7 and 14).

The Rapture? Oh Come *ON!*
So when the Rapture *does* occur (see chapter 5; *The Great Evacuation*), Satan will have already been hard at work creating his own kingdom. With the Church gone, "he who restrains" will also step aside (cf. 2 Thessalonians 2:7). The Holy Spirit? Michael, the Archangel? If the Holy Spirit, He who worked through millions of Christians since the birth of the Church, will move aside and, for a time, there is no one left to directly work through. The gates of hell will open and Satan will literally run rampant, doing nearly anything he sets his mind to doing. The preparations which have been going on behind the scenes since the death and resurrection of Jesus Christ, will finally come into full view. The New Age adherents will finally see their messiah and woe to them because of the great evil he conceals.

While Christians waste time arguing the biblical veracity of events like the Rapture and the Second Coming, this is not the case within the New Age. It seems that most within the New Age movement have no problem with a future event in which millions will disappear off the face of this planet in an instant. Satan has prepared their minds for this event, and it will not take them by surprise. Certainly, the event itself may *shock* them, due to its enormity and instantaneous nature, but as soon as they regain their composure, they will praise the name of their god because now – *finally* – the world and its citizens can advance to the next spiritual plane, with nothing blocking the way.

The New Age movement used to be viewed by most as simply a lovefest made up of hippies, who never outgrew the ideal of envisioning worldwide peace and love. Involved in communal living, and a great deal of meditation, drugs and yoga, they seemed harmless to the rest of the world. Unfortunately, they have become anything but harmless. As the Christian longs for the reward of heaven and an eternity with Jesus, the New Ager longs for the final "Christ's" revealing, in order to watch the ushering in of a new world order.

Early in this country's development, founded by people who had a profound (albeit somewhat confused) view of God, the "*Adventist movement founded by William Miller experienced 'great disappointments' of 1843 and 1844. That movement was based upon the premise that the 'Great Falling Away' or apostasy of Thessalonians had already occurred between the era of Constantine and the Reformation during a 1,260-year period. This 'apostasy' would reveal the 'Man of Perdition,' whom they believed to be the Catholic pope.*"[9] This is one of the dangers, by the way, of allegorizing Scriptures, as evidenced here. These beliefs stem from a purely spiritualized view of the Bible. Nothing has been viewed literally.

Cumby explains that it was not merely the Adventist movement which held this view, but other Protestant denominations believed this as well. At the same time, though, many still believed that the Old Testament prophecies regarding Israel had not yet been fulfilled. It created a bit of a confused, allegorized understanding of prophetic discourse, loosely based on the Bible.

Prophecy Goes Allegorical
The Adventists, who opted to interpret these prophecies in *spiritual* terms, rather than *literal* created not a few problems. "*Interpreting this prophecy to mean a 'spiritual Israel' rather than a political Israel,*

the Adventists felt that all prophecies were fulfilled except for the 'Great Commission' – the command to preach the gospel to all nations."[10]

Of course, eventually history tells us that Israel did once again become a nation. This took place in 1948, and it has been variously interpreted to mean different things, depending upon the group. Some view this as a complete accident of nature. Others believe that it is of God, as things moved toward fulfillment. The problem of course is that ever since then, passions on all sides of the issue have erupted within the church, with people pointing fingers, calling each other names and in general, vilifying those with opposing positions regarding Israel and the potential prophetic nature of its restoration. To those outside the visible Church, this would simply serve to reinforce their view that the Church was made up of a bunch of hypocritical individuals who really had no truth, but knew how to fight with each other.

Cumby explains, *"What nearly every 'Christian' name-caller overlooked were the plain and simply biblical specifications of the spirit of antichrist and the fact that a Movement meeting these specifications was growing under their noses and even influencing their churches."*[11]

The New Age has changed much over the last twenty to thirty years. What we are experiencing now is the last stage of a movement which will culminate with the revelation of the one who Paul describes as the *"man of lawlessness...the son of destruction, who opposes and exalts himself against every so-called god or object of worship, so that he takes his seat in the temple of God, proclaiming himself to be God,"* (2 Thessalonians 1:3b-4).

The End is Coming

It is interesting to consider that both Christians and New Agers are waiting for the culmination of this age. Both groups are waiting for their individual messiahs; the Church awaits the return of Jesus Christ and the New Age awaits the revelation of the Antichrist, thought to be the real Christ. Because of their consistent rejection of authentic salvation, preferring instead to rely on their own strength, their own power and ability, they will get their wish to see if they can become gods. Certainly, they will be encouraged to do so by the Antichrist himself. To eventually bow in worship to him will not seem one bit out of the ordinary. After all, he will be the epitome of what they wish to become and since god is in everything and all is god, to worship him is to worship themselves.

Those who doubt the prophecies regarding the end times, are looking for no one, due to their belief that Christ's return was/is an event taking place within the spiritual realm. They will likely be shocked when the Rapture occurs and possibly before that, a northern attempted invasion into Israel, which will be dealt with by God Himself.

Satan merely *appears* to have his bases covered. He has fooled all the groups that need to be fooled with the perfect lie for each; a lie that convinces each group what *they* believe is the correct belief.

The New Age movement has become a force that the world will reckon with and a force that is fast becoming a spiritual powerhouse, both outside and inside the Church. Ultimately, though, true Christians are aware of the fact that Satan moves only as God allows. His kingdom stands and falls by God's will. The revelation of Maitreya and everything else connected to Satan's plan through the New Age is under God's careful scrutiny and full sovereignty.

It should also be noted that the New Age movement has made serious gains into the visible church, with its ancient mystical practices and idolatry. This will be more fully investigated in our next chapter.

No Worries – God is Sovereign
In spite of what the New Age has become or will evolve into, God is absolutely in command. His throne has never, nor will ever be in jeopardy. The pretenders and wannabes who seek access to His throne

in order to usurp Him, will be shown for who they really are, and the true power that motivates them. They, along with their evil mentor will one day, at the correct, predetermined time will come to a violent and quick end.

The only one standing will be the only true Ruler, God Himself, Jesus Christ, along with those who stand with Him. For that, we praise His Name and look for His coming.

---

[1] Chuck Missler, *Alien Encounters* (Coeur d'Alene: Koinonia House 1997), 144
[2] Constance Cumby, *The Hidden Dangers of the Rainbow* (Shreveport: Huntington House 1983), 7
[3] Ibid, 20
[4] http://www.maitreya.org/ 06/09/2009
[5] Ibid
[6] http://www.maitreya.org/english/third_eye.htm 06/09/2009
[7] http://www.maitreya.org/english/Letters/Leaders/letter_to_leaders.htm 06/09/2009
[8] Ibid
[9] Constance Cumby, *The Hidden Dangers of the Rainbow* (Shreveport: Huntington House 1983), 36
[10] Ibid, 37
[11] Ibid

Chapter 4
All Roads Lead to Rome

It is ironic that in today's society, Christians are finding themselves being labeled "intolerant" and "arrogant." This is because we apparently have the audacity to suggest, or even clearly teach, that there is only *one* way to reach God and that is through the Lord Jesus Christ.

It was His atonement on Calvary's cross that purchased for humanity the opportunity to re-establish a relationship with God. We call this *salvation,* and if not for what Christ accomplished on the cross, that way back to God as salvation would forever remain closed with the failure of Adam and Eve, in Genesis 3.

Authentic Christians Believe What Christ Said

Christians are simply echoing what Jesus said about Himself in John 14:6, *"I am the way, the truth and the life. No one comes to Father but by me the Son."* To everyone who is not a Christian, and has no plans to become one, this statement *is* extremely arrogant. How can there be only *one* way, or *one* truth? History has shown that this cannot be true. Certainly, it cannot be argued that many have seen and do see the truth as being *relative*, morphing as the circumstances merit, into something plausible and, which meets the needs of that particular situation.

In one swell swoop though, not only did Christ negate this errant viewpoint, but He knocked every other pretender to the throne off the table. He was saying, in no uncertain terms, that there is only one salvation and that salvation came only from and through *Him*. It comes from no one else. Every other messiah wannabe was instantly labeled *false* by Jesus.

In fact, if we look back over the historical landscape, there has been no other individual claiming to be the savior, who actually did what Christ did; dying a painfully barbaric, yet innocent death on a cross. He willingly gave Himself over to that undeserved punishment in order that mankind would have the possibility of regaining access to God in relationship. There has been no other individual in all of history who claimed what Christ claimed and did what He did.

In spite of this affirmation of His own qualifications as Savior, many within the world prefer to relegate Jesus to the back of bus, as a good teacher, or wonderful prophet. He is certainly not the only way to God though, they say without hesitation.

However, the unavoidable fact remains that for Jesus to say what He said, not only about Himself, but by implication, about all others, does *not* create a *good teacher*. That Person is either telling the absolute truth, or He is a complete liar. Deciding that Jesus is a good teacher comes somewhere in the middle and in this case, it simply does not fit. If it is true that there are other ways to find God, as many teach today, then Christ's declarative statement, cannot be taken as a good *anything*. It is actually *not* good. It is a terrible statement *if* there are other ways to reach God, then through Jesus Christ.

Oh, the Arrogance!

So the true Christian, because he teaches that salvation comes only through Jesus Christ, is labeled arrogant, or not in harmony with society. This Christian has no clue, people say as they roll their eyes, and smile knowingly to one another. Does this Christian not realize that he is offending every other religion and/or culture by that statement? Does he not realize that he is not making friends with any-one, but creating enemies instead?

The question must be asked, *who does the Christian serve?* Are we really to be concerned about what the world teaches? Are we to be afraid that we might be rejected by the world because what we teach is so *inclusive* and *separating?*

In chapter one of this book, we quoted from one of John MacArthur's books called *Why One Way?* The sad truth of the matter is that Dr. MacArthur is absolutely correct when he asks the question "*Why do evangelicals try so desperately to court the world's favor.*"[1]

Some obviously do this because they do not want their membership or number of attendees to diminish. After all, they have spent months or years building monolithic churches. These facilities are extremely expensive to maintain. A loss in revenue, through a departure of faithful givers would not be good. Others become friends with the world because they actually seem to question the veracity of Jesus' own statement. Did He *really* mean what He said, they wonder?

It is obvious, that for the mega-churches of today, in order to remain afloat financially, large numbers of people are needed; people who give and will continue to give to support salaries, programs, building additions and more. It would not do to take the chance of offending some of these people, who might leave the church and take their wallets with them. What would become of all the programs these churches have begun? What about the many staff members they have hired to run these programs? What about this, or that? How will they survive?

Leaders Going Blind

Unfortunately these leaders have either lost their own vision (if they had one) for what God is doing in the world, or they have only cared about hearing the world's applause from the beginning. That is the temptation with large churches. It becomes a matter of survival, rather than expositional preaching God's Word, in spite of what some may think of it, or react to it.

Actually, in today's modern outlook, it does not even have to be about *salvation* (though it often is). The topic can be homosexuality as we have previously seen, or something else altogether. Each time the true Christian espouses an opinion that is *biblically*-based, and due to that, is seen as being against the current "norm" of society, then that same Christian becomes tagged with the *intolerant* label.

The truth though, is that within society, *someone's* morality will be followed. That morality should benefit as many as possible. However, in the world's lost condition, no morality can benefit everyone, and it becomes personal when someone's own beliefs feel trampled. That is simply part of the problem when the culture is as multi-faceted as the United States has become. The non-Christian feels imposed upon by the Christian. The Muslim feels threatened by the Jew, or the Christian, or western civilization in general. Atheists are bothered by anyone's religious views that impinge upon their freedom to exercise no religion at all, or in any other way, cramp their style.

While moral issues are very important, it is easy to become sidetracked by them, thinking that by merely increasing the level of morality in society, a greater awareness of God is achieved. This then is believed to cultivate conditions that make it easier for people to embrace salvation. There is no biblical principle for this ideology. Christ seemed not to be concerned with the Roman Empire, and the way in which they governed. He was not concerned about their lack of morality or at least the way in which they understood morality. Christ's concern was for the "lost sheep of Israel" and leading them back to the Father (cf. Matthew 10:5-6; Matthew 15:24). In other words, His main concern was to straighten Israel out on her errant understanding of God's Word to them. He wanted them to enjoy the *salvation* they were created to enjoy. He was not blind to the needs of those outside of Israel, but His first priority was for them.

Who would argue that the reason for which Jesus came was for salvation? Everything in His life led to that. He lived a life of sinless perfection, which qualified Him to be the sin offering in order that man might taste the goodness of God, which is only found in His salvation. It was for this purpose that He became a Man, while remaining fully God. We are told that He cried for Jerusalem because of their unbelief (cf. Luke 19: 41-44), but Paul tells us that we are blessed *because* of their unbelief (cf. Romans 11:11-24). It is important that we understand this because it is here that we realize the importance of God's salvation; preaching it, teaching it and living it.

Salvation is what Jesus came to accomplish. His death on Calvary's cross provided that possibility for humanity. His salvation is now available. Is He being truthful when He says that He is the way, the truth and the life? Is He exaggerating His importance by essentially implying that salvation is found in no other individual? Not at all.

It Cannot Be More Than One Way
The road which leads to salvation is what Jesus referred to as the narrow path (cf. Matthew 7:14). He included the word "and few be they

that find it." Jesus was closing every other door. He was sealing up every other avenue that claimed to achieve or obtain salvation for anyone. There was nothing outside of Himself that enabled a person to arrive at the proper gate.

Salvation is certainly the most important issue that every individual faces. How each responds to that issue is literally the difference between eternal life and eternal death. The wrong answer here means death in the afterlife there.

Nevertheless, today, many clearly teach another gospel, or way of salvation. Many suggest or go so far as to state that salvation is found elsewhere, other than Christ.

There are a number of "big" names in the field of religion. Many of those names are also associated with what has become known as the Emergent Church; something that is really nothing more than the New Age in church garb. The Emergent Church has moved into the realm of mysticism and encourages those within these types of churches to do the same. Often the emphasis found within these churches is one that is based on *feeling* (in contrast to opposed to having a better understanding of God's Word). It is in experiencing God that people get to know Him better, we are told by leaders within the Emergent Church. There are often more questions asked than answered as well. The idea is that there may not actually *be* one right answer, so it is better to simply ask questions, bounce ideas around and come to a consensus. The Bible is often pushed off to the side, and it is used as a last resort in many cases.

How You Doin' J-Man?!
The tone of an Emergent Church is *casual*. People dress casually (including the person who oversees the service). The pulpit is normally pushed off to the side, often replaced by a music stand and possibly even a stool or chair is used by the "Overseer" or "host" if you will. From there, a message is presented that normally includes funny

jokes, an upbeat delivery and a verse of Scripture here and there. One easily gets the impression that if Jesus actually appeared in one of these services, the people might think that they could walk right up to Him and shout, "Yo, J-Man. What up!?" with a slap on the back. It seems that what Peter, James and John did as a reaction to the Transfiguration (cf. Matthew 17:1-9, Mark 9:2-8, Luke 9:28-36) is the furthest thing from anyone's mind.

Preaching in these churches is not really preaching as much as it is giving a message. The message is almost always topical; how to have friends, how to break free, how to do this or that. These types of messages emphasize how a person can use God to help themselves get to the next level of whatever level they are trying to get to.

Rock On!
Normally, the music is bright; even rocky, or what some might term worldly. The entire demeanor of these services caters to people who are "seeker sensitive." In other words, these churches are trying to reach out to people who do not yet know Christ. This is certainly good, but unfortunately, by and large, they are not normally teaching them anything about salvation.

Please do not get me wrong. I have played the drums for years, and I do not mind upbeat music. However, it had better be uplifting as well. The trouble is that much of today's so-called Christian music is that in name only. There is very little Christian theology built into many of these songs. The hymns of old, which have a good deal of Scriptural depth to them, have been replaced with feel-good choruses, that have a beat and you can dance to them.

Worship should be just that; *worship* and that is difficult to do if the words are simply feel-good phrases, with music that is much the same. The music and singing should imbue a deep sense of reverence for God. It should not necessarily make you want to dance and jiggle.

Wait. Is Christ the ONLY Way?

Many leaders today within the Emergent Church will actually come out and suggest that maybe Jesus is *not* the only way, or to be more exact, they may say that Christianity is not necessarily the only way, like Tony Campolo has stated in numerous ways:

"I am saying that there is no salvation apart from Jesus; that's my evangelical mindset. However, I am not convinced that Jesus only lives in Christians."[2]

"...what can I say to an Islamic brother who has fed the hungry, and clothed the naked? You say, 'But he hasn't a personal relationship with Christ.' I would argue with that. And I would say from a Christian perspective, in as much as you did it to the least of these you did it unto Christ. You did have a personal relationship with Christ, you just didn't know it."[3]

The above two comments are from Tony Campolo and he is one of those in the forefront of the Emergent Church movement. His comments do not even need to be considered closely to understand that he is saying that Jesus lives in others who are not necessarily people who would be considered Christians, and even within people who are not aware of His presence. Yet, this appears to be in direct opposition to what Jesus Himself said.

The fact that Mr. Campolo believes that Jesus can live in others who are not Christians simply means that he believes there is a salvation that others can experience apart from Christianity. They might be Muslim (as his second comment indicates), or within those who are members of cults, or something else entirely.

He bases this opinion on the fact that these people may have led socially valuable lives, in that they spent time feeding the hungry and clothing the naked. The truth of this particular parable – the Sheep and the Goats – is best seen (like all truth of Scripture) within its context, found in Matthew 25:31–46. There are generally two interpretations of this particular parable. One way to view this is one of the last judgments of Christ after His return to earth, when He sets up His earthly kingdom, after the end of the Great Tribulation.

Christ is judging those nations based on how they took care of the Jews who had just gone through tremendously evil persecution headed by Antichrist. While His basis seems to be judging them on what they *did*, the reality is that only those who had become Christian during the Tribulation/Great Tribulation would have had the proper outlook enough to even want to help Jews since to do so and be caught will likely mean the same retributive response by Antichrist.

The other way of viewing this parable is to see all the individuals as Christians; some who have little or nothing and others who have more. How did those Christians who had more relate to those who had little? In other words, was their faith *real* so that as James would say, their faith was seen in their *action* (James 2:18)?

One Step Forward; Two Steps Back
As Dr. MacArthur relates in his book *Why One Way?*, society has gone beyond Modernism and it has entered into what is termed Postmodernism. *"Postmodernists have repudiated modernism's absolute confidence in science as the only pathway to the truth. In fact, postmodernism has completely lost interest in 'the truth'" insisting that there is no thing as absolute, objective, or universal truth."*[4]

So what once was considered to be truth, has now been replaced by something that leaves truth up for grabs. In that sense, truth has become relative, ultimately to be decided by the individual himself. This subjective view of truth is no different than what existed during Pilate's day, when truth was up for grabs then as well. Because of the proliferation of the Greek and Roman gods and goddesses, truth was seen differently by different people, depending upon their own particular view of a god or gods they worshipped. Our society is fast becoming exactly like this.

Since truth is seen as comparative, with each person subjectively deciding upon its relevance, it is no wonder then that the Christian's "one way" view of salvation is not only seen as antiquated and unenlightened, but as a real problem for those who believe truth is too large to be relegated to one thing.

We Are All Gods

Not long ago, during a special taping of a daytime talk show, a well known hostess had as her guest, another well known individual, within the New Age arena because of a number of books he had written. His books speak of a god in which all participate. In fact, his main message is similar to the messages presented by countless New Age adherents; *we are gods*. What we fail to do is to realize our full potential. Once we realize our full potential, we unlock our own deity within, and the last phase of our salvation will begin.

The interesting thing of course is that within many of these messages, Christian sounding terms are utilized, mainly because of their familiarity. Rather than be off-putting to someone, words like *salvation* or similar terms tend to draw people in because they are already well known to most.

During the course of the show, a question and answer period was provided and one woman stood and essentially said that salvation came only from Jesus Christ and she quoted John 14:6. There were a number of people who agreed with her and showed their agreement by clapping. The nonplussed hostess simply shook her head and replied *"There couldn't possibly be only one way. There couldn't possibly be."*

That of course is sad, but it is the way things are going these days and we can expect more of the same as time moves forward, toward the end. It leads to the question of whether or not there is absolute truth. If there is, then Jesus has a strong argument in His favor. If there is no such thing as absolute truth, then His words of John 14:6 can be ignored, as coming from Someone who really has no clue.

Truth is Just One Variable

For most people today, truth is a variable. It is not uncommon to hear comments that are designed to essentially tell people that a particular truth is fine for them, but others may need a different truth. So begins a long line of subjectivity of truth that looks different for each person.

Why do we do this? The largest reason likely has to do with what Dr. MacArthur stated, which is attempting to be friends with the world. We want to be seen in a favorable light, so we do not want to take the chance of doing things that may ruffle feathers, or offend someone outright.

Yet, this is not the model that Jesus left for us in Scripture. He often took on the religious leaders of His time who had ensnared people by hiding the truth of the gospel under layers of rabbinical teaching and tradition. This hidden truth was extremely difficult for the religious leaders to find, and next to impossible for the average, common person, who relied on the teachings of the Scribes and Pharisees, to understand.

"Authentic Christianity has always held that Scripture is absolute, objective truth. It is as true for one person as it is for another, regardless of anyone's opinion about it. It has one true meaning that applies to everyone. It is God's Word to humanity, and its true meaning is determined by God; it is not something that can be shaped to fit the preferences of individual hearers."[5]

Unfortunately, this is becoming less and less believed and espoused even within the Church today. One must ask how it could be any other way, regarding God's Word? Is it objective truth or not? If not, then one moral rule or law is just as good as another, provided the majority agrees with it. If it is objective, then to circumvent it by trying to create something else entirely, is to not only ignore God and His truth, but to do exactly what Satan has been attempting to do for centuries. Satan lies as a matter of course and he will continue to lie in order to establish what he feels is his rightly deserved throne. But because everything about him involves a lie, then his kingdom will not stand and has, in fact, been defeated already at the cross.

In a day and age where truth is once again becoming tragically relative, authentic Christians stand out like the proverbial sore thumb. We will only have two choices; 1) to attempt to befriend the world, or 2) to remain steadfast with God. It is impossible to do both.

Telling It Like It Is
James takes the bull by the horns, teaching his readers that to have any type of friendship with the world, places us in the position of being *against* God. He is not speaking of our associations with those in the world who are lost. He is speaking of having the *desires* of those who are lost. These people want *things* like money, fast and expensive cars, big homes, lots of food, expensive vacations, and much more. They really do not care who they step on to acquire those things. Certainly James is not arguing that people are not allowed to work hard enough to be able to buy a car, or have enough food for their family, or want to own their own home. James is, instead insisting that those who have these desires *solely* and *primarily* wind up placing themselves in opposition to God.

James clearly brings this out in his epistle, *"What causes quarrels and what causes fights among you? Is it not this, that your passions are at war within you? You desire and do not have, so you murder. You covet and cannot obtain, so you fight and quarrel. You do not have, because you do not ask. You ask and do not receive, because you ask wrongly, to spend it on your passions. You adulterous people! Do you not know that friendship with the world is enmity with God? Therefore whoever wishes to be a friend of the world makes himself an enemy of God. Or do you suppose it is to no purpose that the Scripture says, "He yearns jealously over the spirit that he has made to dwell in us"? But he gives more grace. Therefore it says, "God opposes the proud, but gives grace to the humble." Submit yourselves therefore to God. Resist the devil, and he will flee from you. Draw near to God, and he will draw near to you. Cleanse your hands, you sinners, and purify your hearts, you double-minded. Be wretched and mourn and weep. Let your laughter be turned to mourning and your joy to gloom. Humble yourselves before the Lord, and he will exalt you,"* (James 4:1-10).

Friends to the World

Any Christian who seeks to be friends with world is making a terribly grave mistake. We are not here to befriend the world (cf. 1 John 2:15). We are here to preach the gospel by the example of our lives and the words of our mouth (James 1:22). It is impossible to do this while yearning for what the world has to offer. It cannot be done, yet too many Christians today are trying to do just that.

Christians need to take some time to read through Foxe's Book of Martyrs. It would do us all good. These people stood for God against tremendous persecution, yet they gave no ground. Instead, they preferred to die if necessary than wind up betraying the One who had given His life so that they might have salvation.

We are called out of the world, yet we are still living in the world. In that case, God obviously does not want us to sequester ourselves, trying to make ourselves into an island. He wants to work in and through us as He calls people to Himself, until the fullness of the Gentiles has been established.

These days are difficult. For the first time in our history, we undoubtedly have a president who is Muslim. He is more of a socialist than any president that came before him, and within a short time, it seems that the government, under his leadership, has taken over a number of big businesses and he is now eyeing healthcare. The tragedy is that he won by a landslide. People were either blind to his inner ideals, or they wanted them. Ultimately though, God is the one who put President Obama in office, and He did so, because He has a purpose for him. It is very likely that Obama himself is not aware of any purpose God may have, outside of himself. President Obama has his plan, but God has His, and in the final analysis, it is God's plan which will be accomplished. It is in that vein that Christians must continue to pray daily for our president, that God will protect him and use him for the purposes that God Himself has ordained.

In the meantime, Christians face increasing trials. Because the direction of society is moving further and further away from anything that even remotely resembles objective truth, the true Christian will stand out more and more, or *should*.

"But understand this, that in the last days there will come times of difficulty. For people will be lovers of self, lovers of money, proud, arrogant, abusive, disobedient to their parents, ungrateful, unholy, heartless, unappeasable, slanderous, without self-control, brutal, not loving good, treacherous, reckless, swollen with conceit, lovers of pleasure rather than lovers of God, having the appearance of godliness, but denying its power. Avoid such people. For among them are those who creep into households and capture weak women, burdened with sins and led astray by various passions, always learning and never able to arrive at a knowledge of the truth. Just as Jannes and Jambres opposed Moses, so these men also oppose the truth, men corrupted in mind and disqualified regarding the faith. But they will not get very far, for their folly will be plain to all, as was that of those two men," (2 Timothy 3:1-9).

Tough Times Are Here and Ahead
Paul spoke plainly to Timothy, regarding the difficulties of the End Times, which began with Jesus' resurrection and eventual ascension. He warned Timothy to be aware of the changes that would occur within society; changes that would not be beneficial for anyone and which

would cast the true Christian in the unfavorable light of being seen as intolerant.

We know that Paul in Galatians spoke very harshly about those who would come preaching something else entirely. He said "*But even if we or an angel from heaven should preach to you a gospel contrary to the one we preached to you, let him be accursed. As we have said before, so now I say again: If anyone is preaching to you a gospel contrary to the one you received, let him be accursed.*

For am I now seeking the approval of man, or of God? Or am I trying to please man? If I were still trying to please man, I would not be a servant of Christ," (Galatians 1:8-10).

Cannot Serve God and Money
There are too many within Christendom today who seem to be much more interested in being friends with world than in protecting the gospel of Jesus Christ. They preach another gospel – a gospel based on social change – and encourage others to do the same.

Because some believe for instance, that Jesus lives in others though they are of different religions, solely because they are involved in helping others, one can only wonder where this is stated or implied in Scripture? Surely, this is another gospel; one which mocks Christ's own words of John 14:6 "*I am the way, the truth and the life. No one comes to the Father but by me.*" If it merely takes good works, or helping those within society, then surely the death and shedding of Christ's blood was not needed and He died in vein. Those who hear the true gospel and reject it do not wind up being Christians because they become involved in some social gospel, while remaining part of another religion.

Whom Do You Serve?
In our society, the Christian is seen more and more as *intolerant* because they have the audacity to preach one way of salvation and dare

to suggest that due to sin, all have fallen short of God's glory. The fact that we may do that does not mean we do not see our own sin. It is *because* we see our own see that we are also able to see the sin of others.

Those who refuse to call sin what it is, do a tremendously huge disservice to the gospel of Jesus Christ. In their desire to be seen favorably by the world, they turn the gospel into something it is not. In the meantime, people die and are ushered into hell on a daily basis. These people are no better than the Pharisees, because they keep people from the truth and they themselves will not enter in either. Their reward is seen in what the world gives them, and it is unfortunate that this is quite possibly the only reward they will ever see, or know.

---

[1] John MacArthur, *Why One Way?* (W. Publishing Group 2002), 1
[2] National Liberty Journal, 8/99
[3] http://www.crosscurrents.org/CompoloSpring2005.htm 06/08/2009
[4] John MacArthur, *Why One Way?* (W. Publishing Group 2002), 7
[5] Ibid, 26

Chapter 5
The Great Evacuation

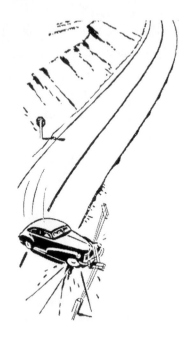

The world is moving onward, seemingly without a care in the world, with the exception of the economy and the continued peace talks in the Middle East. Most believe that these things will work themselves out in time, so they are not too terribly troubled by them. After all, economic cycles, weather patterns and the like come and go. What is interesting though is what is going on in the world *below* the surface. I don't mean in the dirt. I mean, *behind the scenes.*

Many Christians today look forward to an event known in the Bible as the Rapture. The Rapture, spoken about by Paul and implied through the teachings of Christ, is the event in which all who are part of the invisible Church – both living and deceased – are raised to meet Christ in the air (cf. I Thessalonians 4:13-18). Paul's closing words in this section indicate that this occurs in order to avoid the "wrath to come."

The Rapture? That's Just Bunk, Isn't It?

Of course, there is a growing number of Christians who do not at all believe in the Rapture. They look at it as a contrivance by other Christians who are simply afraid to face trials and tribulations. The problem of course with this view is that it does not take into account the trials and tribulations that occur daily in life. Many Christians throughout the world are undergoing severe trials and persecution. Many have lost their lives because of this. Others will likely follow down that path of martyrdom. The argument that the Rapture is simply an "escape clause" really has no merit. Certainly, the truth of a doctrine is not decided on whether or not it seems *plausible*. The truth of it is either confirmed or not in Scripture alone.

Many Christians have spent a good deal of time discussing and arguing over the possibility of the Rapture, leaning on this verse or that to prove or disprove it. At the end of such arguments, people are usually no closer to changing their viewpoints, because both parties firmly believe that they are correct in their belief.

Using the Bible is the best resource to look to when attempting to discern any doctrine espoused by anyone. The true test should always be what is found in God's Word. However, at the same time, with so many people seeing the same passages teaching two different things, it helps to go outside the Bible to see if any verification can be found for such a doctrine as the Rapture.

A Young Gal Named Margaret

In one of the chapters of a previous work titled *The Anti-Supernatural Bias of Ex-Christians (and other important topics)* by the author of this book, the topic of the Rapture was dealt with in light of history. There is a rumor in which it is believed that a young woman named Margaret MacDonald came up with the idea in the mid-1800s. This theory was then shared with her pastor, J. N. Darby, who allegedly ran with it and created an entire doctrine surrounding it.

The chapter responded to the question of the Rapture's true origin, and we were not the first to show from history that the doctrine of the Rapture occurring prior to the Tribulation period, had been espoused by others *before* Margaret MacDonald. Moreover, documentation shows that it was espoused *well before* MacDonald is supposed to have created it. In fact, documents prove that the Rapture (though not named as such) was taught as far back as the 5th or 6th century A.D., and possibly even earlier. This then proved that the Margaret MacDonald rumor is just that; a rumor. For more information, please refer to *The Anti-Supernatural Bias of Ex-Christians*.

In today's society, there are groups who look at life, death, heaven and hell much differently than the average Christian and that has always been the case, since the birth of the Church. In this day and age though, it has become much more noticeable than in years prior. This is at least in part due to the fact that within Christendom, there are those who deny the doctrine of the Rapture, as well as other biblical doctrines related to the End Times. However, with the influx of humanity to the United States in search of safe harbor over the past few decades, new languages, new cultures, and even new religions have come to the fore. These have in essence, questioned the truth of Christianity as never before because of the beliefs they bring with them to these shores.

Couple all of this with the tremendously fast growth of technology, and it is nearly impossible for a person to sneeze in New York City without the rest of the world knowing about it seconds later. Technology has literally put us on the fast track of communication, and precious little time goes by before some piece of news is splashed across web pages on the Internet. Before long, everyone knows of it and are involved in discussions concerning it, if the news is worthy of discussion.

No Going Back

The world has grown to a point of no return. We cannot go back to the days before there were computers, or cell phones, or satellite communication. All of this is here to stay, and it has its good and bad associated with it. It appears that while computers and technology were originally designed to make life easier while increasing productivity, much of what technology offers has in truth become a noose around our necks.

Walk down a street today and see how far you can travel before you find someone talking on their cell phone. Go to a library and see if you can find someone who does not have a laptop with them, hooked up to the Internet and running. Cell phones are not simply devices we use to make phone calls any longer either. Today's cell phone takes pictures, records conversation and video, has many applications that can be downloaded to it and many even come with built in tiny keyboards allowing the owner to create and send text messages more quickly.

Video cameras, once costing thousands of dollars, are now being produced for less than one hundred dollars. While the quality of the video is not of course as good as the higher end models, the low cost puts a video camera in range of just about everyone's budget. Because of this, a proliferation of TV programming focusing on spills, thrills and foibles of John Q. Citizen, crazy drivers, and stupid criminals, fills our TV screens for those who care to watch.

Security cameras are everywhere. It is impossible to go into a store, a mall, even doctors' offices and the like without seeing a video camera recording your actions. Cameras are placed on certain intersections in order to catch drivers going through red lights. Where can one hide from "Big Brother's" watchful eye? While all of these cameras create a sense of security within many, they also remove certain civil rights and freedoms that this country has been known for having. Still, it seems that the majority is willing to make that trade off to have a greater sense of safety while in public.

More and more items today are produced with computerized parts. Cars, TVs, DVD players, phones, microwave ovens, dishwashers, washers and dryers and even tools now have computerized parts and chips in them. This supposedly makes the product work better, yet, they are more pricey because of that. No longer can someone just "tinker" with a product and fix something. It often requires a computer wizard and barring that, replacing the item. Except for products that have no motorized mechanisms, it is difficult to think of an item that is completely devoid of computer technology.

As mentioned, one of the interesting side effects of this type of technology is the ability to transmit and receive information that much more quickly. Go to any of the online free video places where anyone can post a video and every topic under the sun can be located there. These topics extend to the full range of subjects; some that were even either completely downplayed before, or only discussed with other individuals who were of like mind, in order not to be seen as loopy.

ETs and UFOs

One such subject today has to do with extra-terrestrials and UFOs. Years ago, this was a very touchy subject. It just was not discussed by people who were considered to be *normal*. Once someone entered into one of these discussions and signified any type of belief at all in the UFO phenomenon, the person was seen as being a bit *abnormal* and avoided.

However, in the last few decades, a number of things have occurred which have made discussion of UFOs much more acceptable and even credible. No longer are we discussing *little green men* from Mars. People routinely discuss the different species of extra-terrestrial life forms that supposedly have visited, or even *routinely* visit from beyond our solar system.

Professionals Speak Out

In the 1970s, this entire area of discussion really took off and not just by people of whom others would think to be a bit off in their heads. NASA astronauts, think tanks, intellectuals, talk show hosts, commercial airline pilots and many more began including dialogue about intelligent life forms outside of our solar system as being viable, real and they have gone on to state that contact has been made.

Go on the Internet today and it is not at all difficult to find information about the various species of ETs, with simply a few search words, followed by a few clicks. There are essentially six alien species that are "known" by people in the world today:

- Raelians
- Pleadians
- Greys
- Reptilians
- Insectoids
- Venusians

What is even more interesting than simply reading the names of these supposed species, is that they allegedly attempt to accomplish with humans on this planet. The Raelians are said to be beings which are reptile-looking in nature. These are the ones who it is believed do most of the human abductions. While in their captivity, humans are examined and messages are given to the individual from the Raelian via a form of mental telepathy.

Apparently, not much is known about the Pleadians, but the Greys are the ones that we see in drawings, TV programs and movies most often. The movie *Close Encounters of the Third Kind* portrayed this type of alien.

Reptilians are half-human, half-reptile and Insectoids supposedly look like the lovable alien in the movie *ET*. Venusians are beings said to be from the planet Venus. TV shows and a plethora of Sci-Fi movies related to the UFO genre have made it much easier to digest and discuss aspects of what has become known as UFO-logy.

Now, while it is easy to read this and roll the eyes, the most interesting part of this breaks down into two aspects:

1. The folks who believe these beings exist, *really believe* these beings exist and these folks are from all walks of life.
2. The message that is consistently given by these alien life forms is one of a religious nature.

Aliens are Here to Help
If number one did not get your attention, number two should have. If you go to any of the websites on the Internet related to aliens, UFOs and ETs (along with other unexplained phenomena), you can read for yourself many of the stories and narratives that have been reported. Beyond this, there are snapshots of photos purportedly highlighting some type of UFO craft. Videos can often be found as well. Certainly, some of these are faked (but very good fakes), but there are some that even the experts have not been able to legitimately dismiss, so the jury is still out.

If time is taken to talk personally with these individuals (I have not), or read articles which contain interviews with some of these people, it becomes obvious that these people cannot be merely dismissed out of hand. They are sincere, they are intelligent and they firmly believe that they have had some type of experience (if they were abducted by aliens).

There have been any number of books published on the topic of alien abductions, or things of a similar nature. Many seem to be published by people that might be called "crackpots," or those simply hoping to make a fast buck. Other publications are not so easy to ignore, while others have a good deal of believability to them.

One such book is published by Koinonia House and is co-written by Chuck Missler and Mark Eastman. They have a good deal to say about the possibilities behind this burgeoning alien trend.

There have been documented (some with video) evidence of huge UFO events over the past three to four decades. A number of these videos are easily found on the Internet. The event of January 1, 1993 in Mexico City is one such occurrence. It was reported that on that day, *"a silvery craft [was seen by thousands] performing aerial acrobatics over the central portion of Mexico City in broad daylight."*[1]

UFOs Abound
Missler indicates that later that same day, other craft arrived to join the first one. Again, in this particular instance, thousands of people saw the event and many recorded it. Since the early 90s, UFO sightings have increased tremendously. It is almost as if the aliens (if they actually exist), *want* to be noticed.

In 1996, over Israel, there occurred another UFO sighting. Apparently, this particular UFO simply hovered near the city of Tel Aviv for a while, then began doing tremendous aerial acrobatics, the speed and dexterity with which this object was able to accomplish this cannot apparently be replicated by any known technology today.

As we continue in through the 90s, we see more and more eye-witness accounts of UFOs appearing in the sky in various parts of the world. Beyond this, there has also been a huge upsurge in alien abduction claims. Missler's book lists many of these incidents and the reader is encouraged to avail themselves of not only Chuck's book (information listed at the end of this chapter), but also other books that provide additional corroboration.

You may be wondering why this chapter is even in this book. The truth of the matter is that it may very well be that these aliens are not really "aliens" in the strict sense of the word; the way in which we commonly use the word, referring to beings from other worlds. These beings may in fact be spirit beings we often refer to as *demons*, who, as part of a growing worldwide deception, are disguising themselves as aliens from other worlds. Many of the so-called messages that abductees have received from them are nearly the same and they almost always include the sense that these aliens want nothing more than to *help* us and our world. This has become the standard tune of these beings, as reported by countless abductees.

It appears that in their desire to help us, these aliens also come to us with a warning; a warning that if not heeded, would mean the earth's ultimate demise. In some ways of course, this sounds overly dramatic, and very much like an episode of Star Trek®, or Star Wars®, or some other sci-fi program of similar nature. The problem though is that this is *not* a TV program or movie. The situation as understood or seen by many people, is *real* in nature, and that reality continues to grow as that global group of abductees becomes larger as time goes by.

Pardon My Prodding
So according to many people who say they have been abducted, examined, poked, prodded and given messages (telepathically), the underlying communication to the citizens of earth is that these aliens are coming to visit us more and more because of their concern for our welfare. They are concerned because they do not want us to destroy ourselves. They are concerned because they also want to ensure that we get to the next *evolutionary* level. This is what they *say* as they begin to transmit their messages to us, from their brain to ours. Here then is where it becomes interesting.

Missler clarifies for us. *"One might expect that such a visitation from our "space parents" would be accompanied by detailed information on how to solve our increasing global difficulties. With their supposed highly advanced technology, surely they would have solved the kinds of political, economic, environmental, and medical problems we now face. And yet, no such message [has been] given. Instead, Rael [a person so-*

named by the visiting aliens – ed.] was given a religious message – in effect, a Bible study conducted by an ET!"[2]

What Is There Message?

That is interesting, isn't it? Here we are on earth, with poverty-stricken nations, disease running rampant, seeming insurmountable economic difficulties, no cure for cancer, AIDS, or the common cold, yet these aliens seem not to have anything to offer about those things. Instead they are intent upon explaining the *real* meaning of the Bible to at least some of the abductees.

Missler continues; "*The primary message that the extraterrestrials wanted Rael to understand was that they created mankind. According to Rael, the extraterrestrials told him that they created humanity in their image by sophisticated genetic engineering techniques.*"[3] Rael continues in his book titled *The Message Given to Me by Extraterrestrials*, by explaining and describing the *actual* story of Creation, not the one most of us have read and know found in the first few chapters of Genesis.

If all this is not interesting enough, we find that another one of the main messages being given to earthlings by aliens is one which might cause fear in many, at first glance. This message, if not for the fact that it has been distilled through several individuals on earth at various times, would be extremely difficult to believe. Yet, here is a message given by ETs and recorded in *The Ashtar Command, Project World Evacuation, 1993*: "*Our rescue ships will be able to come in close enough in the twinkling of an eye to set the lifting beams in operation in a moment. And all over the globe where events warrant it, this will be the method of evacuation. Mankind will be lifted, levitated shall we say, by the beams from our smaller ships. These smaller craft will in turn taxi the persons to the larger ships overhead, higher in the atmosphere, where there is ample space and quarters and supplies for millions of people.*"[4]

What was that?! An evacuation of "millions of people"? These series of Ashtar Command messages transmitted to a person named *Tuella* is on the Internet and can be easily read by going to the URL listed at the end of this chapter. The entire book starts out with this small disclaimer: *"Although these Messages of the coming Earth Changes and Ascension of Planet Earth given by the Ashtar Command in the 1980's through Tuella (Thelma Terrell) have since been long delayed in their outcome, mainly through the strong efforts of the Forces of Darkness to eliminate or postpone the event, the instruction and program contained therein remains largely unchanged and applicable to the now fast approaching times of final cleansing."*[5]

The Upcoming Evacuation

Notice what is being stated here. Apparently, these messages were originally transmitted in the 1980s. It was thought then (by the "aliens") that what they were stating was going to come to pass soon. It did not, so this disclaimer was placed as an excuse. The average individual however, will look at this and say "See? It's the Forces of Darkness that are working against world peace! We've got to work *harder!"*

According to Missler, the first messages from the Ashtar Command arrived in 1952 to author George Van Tassel. *"We are concerned about [humanity's] deliberate determination to EXTINGUISH HUMANITY AND TURN THIS PLANET INTO A CINDER...Our missions are peaceful, but this condition occurred before in this solar system and the planet Lucifer was torn to bits. We are determined that it shall not happen again."*[6]

What is engrossing here is that if we compare this with the biblical picture, we gain some insight into what these beings know. In spite of the fact that many within Christendom do not believe in the doctrine of the Rapture, here is a *type* of Rapture being postulated by aliens!

1) The fact that these aliens have already sent messages about a coming evacuation of millions of people from this planet is obviously their

attempt to downplay the Rapture. The Rapture according to the Bible is the instantaneous *translation* of true Christians, who make up the invisible Church. This will happen in a moment, in the twinkling of an eye. Paul speaks of this event in 1 Thessalonians 4:15-17: *"...the Lord himself will descend from heaven with a cry of command, with the voice of an archangel, and with the sound of the trumpet of God. And the dead in Christ will rise first. Then we who are alive, who are left, will be caught up together with them in the clouds to meet the Lord in the air, and so we will always be with the Lord."* This is also reflected in Christ's own Olivet Discourse found in Matthew 24:29-31.

Here we see in a message purportedly transmitted *by* an alien from the Ashtar Command *to* a human being, that these aliens were preparing the earth for a time in which millions of people would vanish instantly from the face of the earth.

So We're the Bad Guys?

Thelma Terrell, (or Tuela as she is known in New Age circles), carried on where Van Tassel left off. *"In the 1980s Ashtar clarified the message to Earth through a new channeler named Thelma Terrell...she compiled the channeled messages of Ashtar, who declared that planet Earth would be spared certain annihilation by an extraterrestrial evacuation of millions of people who* **threaten the harmony and evolution of Earth** *(emphasis added)."*[7]

Ah, so it becomes clearer. First we learn that the aliens have transmitted messages as early as 1952, which tell of a removal of millions of people from the earth, all in the same instant. Then in the 1980s, another person by the name of Tuela, who has apparently replaced the deceased Van Tassel, receives clarified information from this same source that the people who are to be removed are those that threaten earth's existence.

What is fascinating of course, is that all of this sounds like the Rapture to me. It is a fact that Satan knows the Bible and he likely knows it better than any other living human being (besides Christ Himself). During Christ's temptation in the wilderness, Satan quoted Scripture – the Word of God – just as he had in the Garden of Eden. He quoted it in the same manner, slightly twisting the meaning of it, so that while it resembled its original meaning, it now meant something else.

Jesus did not buy any of it, rejecting Satan's advances with Scripture of His own. Satan's deceptive ploys were not strong enough to remove Jesus off the chosen path. The reader is encouraged to read this narrative of Jesus' bout with Satan, and His victory of the same (Matthew 4, Mark 1, and Luke 4).

Satan Knows the Rapture *Will* Occur
Are the powers of Darkness, led by Satan himself, fully aware of an event that Paul speaks of in which all true believers (both dead and alive at the time), will be *caught up*, to be forever with the Lord? It would appear so, but notice that in Satan's version of this event, those who are "raptured" or evacuated off the planet are the *problem* children. It is these folks who are keeping the *rest* of the population and the world itself from evolving into the next stage of existence.

It is not merely Chuck Missler and Mark Eastman that provide us with information that seems to indicate a Rapture-like event of the true Church will occur in the future. Others like Constance Cumby (refer to chapter three), have also written about the New Age Movement, critiquing the new world order that New Agers long for and look forward to becoming a reality. This new world order may very well include aspects of Neo-Nazism, along with solid components of the New Age Movement, which is sadly already finding its way into many mainline churches and denominations.

Referring to this possible future event Christians call the Rapture, one New Age writer states this, "*The people who leave the planet during the time of Earth changes do not fit in here any longer, and they are stopping the harmony of Earth. When the time comes that perhaps 20 mil-*

lion people leave the planet at one time there will be a tremendous shift in consciousness for those who are remaining."[8]

On the Share International website, Benjamin Crème is noted as *"a messenger of hope."*[9] He is called this due to his connection with the spirit world and his ability to channel the "Masters," of which have ultimately become known to Crème as the Hierarchy of the Masters.

In the late 1950s, after having spent a number of years studying the writings of Blavatsky, Alice Bailey and others, Crème began receiving what he called transmissions from these Masters. The first of these transmissions informed Crème of an eventual appearance of Maitreya, or the Christ, of whom Crème referred to as *"Head of our planetary Hierarchy."*[10]

Between the years of 1959 and 1974, the transmissions occurred with some regularity and Crème became deep friends with the one he called simply, the Master. This individual taught Crème things about life, reincarnation, the hierarchy, the higher consciousness and everything connected with the New Age Movement, and coming new world order that he had *not* learned through the writings of Blavatsky and Bailey.

Not long afterward, Crème began having meetings with others of like mind, to introduce them to the world of the New Age Movement and the coming changes that would occur on this planet. A few years after he began these meetings he received another transmission, but instead of it coming from his Master, this one apparently came directly from Maitreya himself. Crème relates this event; *"In June 1974 began a series of overshadowing and transmitted messages by Maitreya, inspiring us, and keeping us informed of the progress of his externalisation. We were privileged also to become aware of the gradual creation and perfectioning of his body of manifestation — the Mayavirupa. In the period from March 1976 to September 1977, these communications from Maitreya became very frequent indeed."*[11]

This was not to be the only message from Maitreya either. There were many more; *"Between September 1977 and June 1982, British author and lecturer Benjamin Crème received a series of 140 Messages from Maitreya, the World Teacher."*[12]

Satan's Hands Are Tied Because of God's Sovereignty

In message number 140, transmitted in May of 1982, Maitreya stated this (in part) through Crème: *"It has been My intention to reveal Myself at the earliest possible moment, to brook no delay, and to come before the world as your Friend and Teacher. Much depends on My immediate discovery, for in this way can I help you to save your world. I am here to aid and teach, to show you the path to the future, and to reveal you to each other as Gods."*[13]

One of the questions that must be asked is twofold; what is keeping the future evacuation from occurring and what is stopping Maitreya from making himself known to the world? In reality, there is only one thing that keeps these events from taking place.

Satan is *not* all-knowing, or all-powerful. He cannot be in more than one place at the same time. Apart from all these things, he does *not* know every detail about the future. He only knows what he sees in the Bible. As I have stated in another book I have written (*Dispensationalism's View of God's Sovereignty*), this is one of the largest reasons why God has chosen to have *progressively* revealed His will to humanity. The more God revealed to humanity, the more Satan knew, so God kept many things close to His chest so to speak. He only revealed things as He saw fit and only what mankind needed to know at that moment. Yes, man was in the dark about any number of things, but so was Satan.

Satan Reads the Bible

Because Satan only knows what he learns through the revelation of Scripture, along with what he sees God actually doing, he does not know the day or the hour of many events which are said to be connected to the End Times. If the Rapture is slated to occur, as we believe the Bible teaches it will, no one knows exactly *when* that event will occur. The exact day and hour is not listed in Scripture. The closest we get to it is when Jesus speaks of the times nearing the Great Tribulation in Matthew 24. He speaks of the fact that His disciples knew when the seasons were changing by looking at the trees. It is by that change that we know one season blends into another. In the same way, Christ gave us clues or signs to look for which would signal the *beginning* of the end.

As Fruchtenbaum states in *Footsteps of the Messiah,* as far as the Jewish rabbis of old were concerned, there were simply two ages; this age and the age to come. In Matthew 24, when Christ speaks of the end of the age, He is referring to the end of *this* age, which is controlled by *man's rule* (but of course, overseen by God). This age will end, when Jesus returns physically to set up His kingdom on earth, and will also physically rule from David's throne in Jerusalem. This is what separates this age from the next; Christ's return.

The signs Jesus spoke of in the Olivet Discourse were given to serve as a way to keep track of things and to watch for as this age began to wind down. Much speculation, argumentation and debate about what Jesus meant has raged on. Within the past few decades, the belief that most prophetic events have already occurred in the past, leaving only a few chapters in the last part of Revelation to occur has gained momentum. This is at least part of the reason I included this chapter, because the modern trend in much of the visible Church, believes that Christ's return, far from being the physical return that the two "men" in Acts 1 pointed to, was *spiritual* in nature and occurred in A.D. 70 with the destruction of Jerusalem and the Temple.

This belief seems to stem from Scripture, but in truth, what many Christians today are advocating is a *gradual improvement* in society. Once we wipe out famine, disease and the like, man himself will be much improved. This improvement will by itself, usher in a new form of spiritual Christianity; one in which Christ as the absolute head of the Church, will be able to reign from heaven through *all* creatures on earth. Unfortunately as stated, this is in marked contrast with what the Bible teaches and the literal meaning that stems from that teaching.

Spiritual Fulfillment?
In his book *Satan His Motives and Methods*, Lewis Sperry Chafer pointed out then (in 1919), that a belief in a spiritual form of fulfillment had taken place by Christ. This of course was at odds with the orthodox evangelical position, which looked to the yet future physical return of Jesus. has this to say regarding this modern belief;
"Well may believers study their own motives in service in view of these vastly differing programs; and question whether there is in them a humble willingness to cooperate in the present purpose of God in preparing the Bride for the returning King. Or whether, on the other hand, they have carelessly fallen in with the Satanic ideal which rejects the coming kingdom of Christ by an unholy attempt to establish the present kingdom of Satan."[14]

So on one hand, we see humanity – including many within the visible Church – catering to the ideas presented by the enemy that if we all work hard enough, we will one day attain that which we long for in Christ. It is unfortunate that these people are blinded to the truth of the Bible, with its plain, clear message of future events.

Those of us who receive the message of His Word plainly, understanding its meaning in literal terms, look for the signs that Christ spoke of in His Olivet Discourse. While these signs do not necessarily pinpoint the exact timing of future events, they let us know whether or not the beginning of birth pains has already begun, or is yet future. We see these signs as simply that; *indicators* allowing us to see the progression of things to their chosen culmination.

Satan does the same thing. Through his demonic horde, he keeps abreast of what is going on throughout the world, and attempts to judge the times and seasons, but that is the best he can do. He does not know when the Rapture will occur and for that matter does not know when many other events will occur, which are related to the End Times. This is why he constantly has to "correct" or "clarify" things as time moves onward, through his messengers, leaving unfulfilled the things he transmitted years before, to unknowing and deceived human beings.

New Age Knows What Many Christians Deny
What we know, is that the New Age Movement believes that one day, due to "ignorance" and "an inability to evolve," millions of people will be suddenly and instantly removed from the face of this planet. Satan has made preparation for this upcoming event, by announcing it ahead of time, but simply putting a completely different twist on it.

If the event simply occurred, with absolutely no notice given to humanity, it is likely that at least some people would remember being taught about it from the Bible. They would panic realizing that the Bible prophecy concerning the Rapture had actually occurred! They *were* in point of fact, left behind.

This would not work for Satan's plan at all. He would have to do something to draw attention from the fact that this concept is taught in Scripture. He has a number of choices at his disposal, both of which he seems to have done:

1. **For Christians (professing and true)**: Create doubt within them, so that they themselves do not believe the Rapture will occur. Have them focus on the rumor that Margaret MacDonald actually created the concept. If there are Christians who literally deny that the Rapture is going to occur, then this is what they will teach to everyone; those who believe it and those who do not believe it.

2. **For the Non-Christians (New Agers):** Get the word out way ahead of time the Rapture *will* occur, however the Bible has it wrong. The Rapture will take place to remove Christians from the world, but as far as the world will understand it, these Christians are seen as trouble makers; those who are keeping the planet and people from evolving to the next level.

Satan's Version of the Rapture

Certainly, this is one reason why Satan began to disseminate his own version of the event of the Rapture. He *knows* without doubt that it *will* take place, unlike many Christians today, who deny a good deal of the, as yet unfulfilled, prophetic discourse. Some Christians to be sure, are not in rebellion to God, nor do they desire to work against Him, but they are blind to His purposes related to the End Times. It is because of this that they *do* wind up inadvertently working against Him and His purposes. They do not envision a coming Rapture and many do not envision a coming Great Tribulation either, having sequestered the latter to the A.D. 70 event of Jerusalem's destruction.

Satan on the other hand, knows the Rapture will occur. He knows the Great Tribulation will occur and it is for this event that he is directing much of his energy and power. It is during this time, that Satan will reveal himself to the world through the Antichrist, as a kind, intelligent, loving, tolerant man who because of these things will rise to rule the entire world through a global government of Absolute Imperialism.

Though Satan is working toward the final showdown that will occur at the end of the Great Tribulation, he does not know *when* either the Rapture, or the Great Tribulation will actually occur. These times are in God's hands only and it will only be when that time arrives, will the Rapture of the Church occur. After that, the beginning of the Great Tribulation (comprising a full seven years), will start when the Antichrist is able to gain the trust of Israel, entering into a covenant with her for the seven years of the Tribulation/Great Tribulation.

The Rapture According to Satan

"professing themselves wise, they became as fools" Romans 1:22

FOR NEW AGERS:

People are being told that sometime in the future, an evacuation of millions of people will occur in the "twinkling of an eye." These people are said to keep the planet and its citizenry from evolving to the next level. Their removal means progression for the planet.

"scoffers will come in the last days" 2 Peter 3:3

FOR DOUBTERS:

These folks believe rumors like Margaret MacDonald started the Rapture story and Darby ran with it. Others believe that the Rapture was created by people who are merely looking for a persecution escape clause, or a fast way to make a quick buck.

Ever watchful, Satan continues to keep tabs on everything that happens in this world that he has no control over. This allows him to judge the times and seasons, but as we have seen, though that is not enough, it is the best he can do.

Maitreya Clarifies...and Clarifies
Even when things are clarified by Maitreya or some other entity, as to why, for instance, the great planetary evacuation has not yet taken place, or why Maitreya himself has been unable to reveal himself, the blame is placed on those with *bad energy*. Because these things are happening as spoken of through theses transmissions given over the space of twenty or thirty years, it is stated or implied that those who *keep things* from happening are the problem people of this world. So then, instead of doubting Maitreya's power and ability, eyes turn instead to the *problem* to see what can be done about that.

Within the New Age Movement, the concept of *energy* – both positive and negative – is *foundational*. Those having a positive energy are enabled to move things forward to the next evolutionary phase. Those with a negative energy (read: *Christians*), keep things *from* happening the way the New Age adherents have been told it is scheduled to happen.

One day, as has been noted, according to New Age beliefs, space ships will park themselves above our skies, out of sight. Then, at the appointed time, they will literally vacuum the earth of that which keeps the planet and the people on it from entering a new phase of reality. Thus, the problem of earth's inability to rise to the next level of evolution will have been dealt with once and for all. Nothing then would continue to stand in the way of earth's advancement.

Where Will They Go?
What is to be done with all these millions of people who are instantly whisked away from the planet? We look again to Chuck Missler, who quotes from the spring 1994 issue of *Connecting Link Magazine* from

an article written by Kay Wheeler. Wheeler provides clarification on this upcoming event when millions in an instant will wind up missing. She states, *"Many of these beings who are leaving this planet at this time have completed that which they came to do. It is a time of great rejoicing for them. Do not feel sad about their leaving. They are going home. Many are waiting to be with them again...Many beings must move on, for their thought patterns are of the past. They hold on to these thoughts that keep Earth held back."*[15] Notice how Wheeler has *softened* the blow a bit here. While she states that these individuals are holding the Earth back from its natural evolutionary advancement, she intones that these humans (referred to as "beings") are going to a better place, so while the world should experience a collective sigh of relief, it should also revel in the fact that these missing people are going to a better place.

Truth from a Liar?

I find that especially interesting, because what Wheeler is describing is exactly what the Christian longs for as they look to Christ for the fulfillment of it. In looking closely at what Wheeler has stated, there is a good deal of truth in it, however the beings that have revealed this information to Wheeler want her to understand *not* that the people Raptured off the planet are going to be with Jesus. He is not even mentioned at all. They want her to understand that this future event is all part of their specific evolutionary path; a path in which they will:

1. *Rejoice*
2. *Go home*
3. *Be reunited with loved ones*

This is the perfect picture of what the Christian will experience once this life is left behind. We know that Satan is a liar and the hordes of demons lie as he lies, taking their cue from him. To mix truth with their lies is what comes naturally to them and if it brings about their chosen ends, all the better.

Satan goes on the offensive where the Rapture is concerned. Those within the church who deny that the Rapture is a biblical doctrine have obviously not been paying attention. While they are arguing over meaning of passages of Scripture, they have missed a very large indicator that the Bible is true. Satan and his cohorts have been telling those lost individuals who have become firmly established in the New Age Movement that such an event *will* occur. They have, however, given it their own special meaning.

The question then regarding the possibility of the Rapture is simply this: if the Rapture was/is truly a doctrine of devils with absolutely no biblical basis as some charge, then what possible reason would Satan have in creating any kind of deception surrounding it? If it is not in danger of taking place at all, why would he bother with it? It would be one thing to create that false teaching simply to confuse Christians and get them arguing with one another. It is quite another thing altogether to teach *non-believers* the concept of a Rapture-like event that will occur in the future.

Wasted Effort?
To create a scenario with this amount of detail, related to what *will* happen (but won't), when the Rapture takes place, so that it is seen as something else entirely, would not only be counter-productive to his goals and purposes, but worse than that, makes him appear as someone who really has no clue about what is happening, if the Rapture was not going to actually occur. Certainly, he would not directly be affected negatively, but his plan would and those through whom he is working and speaking would immediately lose all of their credibility. It simply makes absolutely no sense for Satan to create such a charade based around an event that is *not* in the least biblical. On the other hand, if the Rapture *is* slated to occur as the Bible teaches, then Satan has a very good reason for trying to create a diversion by teaching that what is happening is not a biblical event, but one that has to do with the earth's advancement on the evolutionary timeline.

The Rapture and the Second Coming

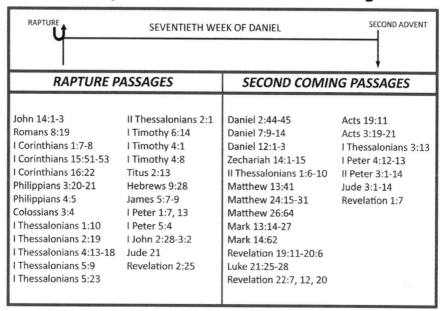

RAPTURE PASSAGES		SECOND COMING PASSAGES	
John 14:1-3	II Thessalonians 2:1	Daniel 2:44-45	Acts 19:11
Romans 8:19	I Timothy 6:14	Daniel 7:9-14	Acts 3:19-21
I Corinthians 1:7-8	I Timothy 4:1	Daniel 12:1-3	I Thessalonians 3:13
I Corinthians 15:51-53	I Timothy 4:8	Zechariah 14:1-15	I Peter 4:12-13
I Corinthians 16:22	Titus 2:13	II Thessalonians 1:6-10	II Peter 3:1-14
Philippians 3:20-21	Hebrews 9:28	Matthew 13:41	Jude 3:1-14
Philippians 4:5	James 5:7-9	Matthew 24:15-31	Revelation 1:7
Colossians 3:4	I Peter 1:7, 13	Matthew 26:64	
I Thessalonians 1:10	I Peter 5:4	Mark 13:14-27	
I Thessalonians 2:19	I John 2:28-3:2	Mark 14:62	
I Thessalonians 4:13-18	Jude 21	Revelation 19:11-20:6	
I Thessalonians 5:9	Revelation 2:25	Luke 21:25-28	
I Thessalonians 5:23		Revelation 22:7, 12, 20	

15 Contrasting Events of the Second Coming

RAPTURE/BLESSED HOPE	GLORIOUS APPEARING
1) Christ comes in air for His own	1) Christ comes with His own to earth
2) Rapture/translation of all Christians	2) No one translated
3) Christians taken to Father's House	3) Resurrected saints do not see Father's House
4) No judgment on earth at Rapture	4) Christ judges inhabitants of earth
5) Church taken to Heaven at Rapture	5) Christ sets up His kingdom on earth
6) Rapture imminent	6) Glorious appearing cannot occur for 7 years
7) No signs for the Rapture	7) Many signs for Christ's physical coming
8) For believers only	8) Affects all humanity
9) Time of joy	9) Time of mourning
10) Before the Day of Wrath (Tribulation)	10) Immediately after Tribulation (Matthew 24)
11) No mention of Satan	11) Satan bound in Abyss for 1,000 years
12) The Judgment Seat of Christ	12) No time or place for Judgment Seat
13) Marriage of the Lamb	13) His bride descends with Him
14) Only His own see Him	14) Every eye will see Him
15) Tribulation can begin	15) 1,000-year kingdom of Christ begins

The Rapture is a biblical event. It is clear not only from Scripture, but from what the enemy of our souls is telling those who are caught in the web of his lies and deceit. The last thing Satan wants the average, unsaved person to know is the *truth* concerning the Rapture. That will not do at all. Better they see this upcoming event as something *he* designed (through those appearing as aliens), for the good of this planet and the good of humanity. He gains much by also having Christians come to disbelieve in the veracity of the Rapture doctrine.

The charts on the previous page highlight passages referring to the Rapture and Second Coming (based on Fruchtenbaum's book *Footsteps of the Messiah*). The top chart compares passages of Scripture connected with the Second Coming to those connected with the Rapture. The bottom chart compares and contrasts the events themselves and as can be seen, there are many differences between these two events.

The charts were created by the author and are based on information from the book by Dr. Arnold G. Fruchtenbaum, *The Footsteps of the Messiah.* The reader is encouraged to study the various sections of Scripture listed in each to determine just exactly what these differences are between the two events. Beyond this, for a complete detailing of these two events, the aforementioned book by Dr. Fruchtenbaum is a must for anyone's library.

The chart below (also based on Fruchtenbaum's book *Footsteps of the Messiah*), outlines the *Promise of the Rapture*, the *Program of the Rapture* and the *Timing of the Rapture*. The clear teaching of Scripture designates a specific event in which all who are in Christ (the Church), are translated, or *caught up* to be with Him in the clouds. This event, unlike the Second Coming, is *not* a return of Christ to earth. In this event, He merely steps away from His throne, out of the third heaven and *greets* His Bride as His Bride is translated.

This event is also very similar to the way Enoch was *translated* prior to the judgment of the global flood in Genesis 4. Enoch walked with God and *"was not because the Lord took him."* Enoch then, was removed from this earth alive. He did *not* see death. This is the exact sense in which Christ's Bride, having already been purified due to His shed blood on Calvary's cross, is caught up to be with Him forever. Many people today teach that the Church needs to be purified before we are able to be presented to Him blameless. This is a false teaching. Paul teaches that there is therefore <u>now</u> NO condemnation to those who are in Christ Jesus (Romans 8:1). For the Christian, there should be no fear in standing before Jesus Christ in judgment (for our salvation).

The Church Awaits for the Last Gentile

The Church awaits the *fullness of the Gentiles* (cf. Romans 11), which is the time we are now living. During this phase, God continues to call out those earmarked for salvation from every nation and culture. When the last of these has been called out, the fullness of the Gentiles will have been reached. The reader is encouraged to read through the passages highlighted in the charts seen on the previous pages.

In a day and age when people are balking at the doctrine of His return, it is important to honestly understand what the Bible teaches. Is the Rapture grounded doctrinally in His Word, or is it a figment of someone's overworked imagination. Because of what the New Age is teaching throughout its loose knit network of adherents, it would appear that Satan knows the Rapture will occur. It is because of this that he has taken the time to thoroughly indoctrinate his followers with the truth of the Rapture, but with his own special twist. It certainly seems to be working.

---

[1] Chuck Missler, *Alien Encounters* (Coeur d'Alene: Koinonia House 1997), 12
[2] Ibid, 136
[3] Ibid, 136
[4] http://www.thenewearth.org/ASHTAR1ProjectWorldEvacuation.html - 06/05/2009
[5] Ibid
[6] Chuck Missler, *Alien Encounters* (Coeur d'Alene: 1997), 187
[7] Ibid, 187
[8] Barbara Marciniak, *Bringers of the Dawn*
[9] http://www.share-international.org/background/bcreme/bc_main.htm 06/05/2009
[10] Ibid
[11] Ibid
[12] http://www.share-international.org/maitreya/messages/Ma_mess.htm 06/05/2009
[13] Ibid
[14] Lewis Sperry Chafer, *Satan His Motives and Methods* (Grand Rapids: Kregal 1990), 67-68
[15] Chuck Missler, *Alien Encounters* (Coeur d'Alene: Koinonia House 1997), 189

Chapter 6

Green! Green! Let's Go Green!

Today, we are hearing more and more about going *green*; the new *environmental* catchphrase. The idea behind this is that we should use less and less of our natural resources, and recycle what we do use, and only purchasing products that have been recycled. One website boasts this phrase, "*the call letters for going green is (sic) RRR – reduce, reuse, recycle.*"[1] Of course, in many respects this is important to conserve and frugally use what is *needed*.

The problem with this outlook is that it tends to reduce the importance of humanity, and increase the importance of everything else.

Proof of this is seen in the way the environmental agencies work. They emphasis is often on saving resources for *future generations*, instead of having the ability to use them now.

A Form of Godliness
While this *appears* to have a form of godliness attached to it, what is actually being done is turning the natural use of God's Creation upside down, so that man is on the bottom of the heap so to speak, with everything else *above* man in significance. In this way, through these ideals, man then is reduced to something which is far less than what God intended him to be.

For instance, in our efforts to save certain species, man then goes without. Because of this, people in various parts of the world wind up starving because it becomes verboten to kill a particular animal. We must save all the trees, so people then, are put out of work. We cannot use the oil off the shore of many parts of the United States because drilling for it *may* pose a danger to sea life. Due to this, the United States has become tethered to foreign countries, which raise or lower the price of oil per barrel at whim.

Dr. MacArthur's Message
At the 2008 Shepherd's Conference, held at Grace Community Church in Los Angeles, Dr. John MacArthur was speaking on this very topic. At one point in his message, he made the statement "*Kill a deer, walk on the grass, and drill for oil.*" The truth is that society has come to see each of these things as *counter-productive* to growth. Yet, the real truth is that – as Dr. MacArthur stated later on in his message – God gave us all of these things for our *benefit*. In the first part of Genesis, God told Adam and Eve to be fruitful and multiply and *subdue* the earth (cf. Genesis 1:28-30). After the global flood which destroyed all the living of Creation, with the exception of Noah, his family and the animals brought into the Ark, God gave the same essential message to Noah and his family (cf. Genesis 9).

God's Words to Adam and Eve are clear: "*Be fruitful and multiply and fill the earth and subdue it and have dominion over the fish of the sea and over the birds of the heavens and over every living thing that moves on the earth.' And God said, 'Behold, I have given you every plant yielding seed that is on the face of all the earth, and every tree with seed in its fruit. You shall have them for food. And to every beast of the earth and to every bird of the heavens and to everything that creeps on the earth, everything that has the breath of life, I have given every green plant for food'. And it was so,*" (Genesis 1:28b-30).

God gave us this planet as our greatest *resource*. We are to *subdue* it, *use* it, have *dominion* over it, <u>*and*</u> *benefit* from it. As good stewards of what God has given us, it is important to conserve and not waste, we have unfortunately gotten to a point in society where animals have become more important than humanity. We are afraid of actually using aspects of the earth and the resources contained within it, because we might use them up. Beyond all of this, we are fearful of destroying this earth, or at the very least, leaving little for future generations.

Man Cannot Destroy the Earth!

The biblical reality is that this earth will *only* be destroyed when God Himself destroys it, as outlined in the one of Peter's epistles and elsewhere (2 Peter 3:10, 12). God has a plan for this earth. He created it *for* human use and consumption. He provided us not only with every herb bearing tree, but with animals, and fish and birds; all for our use to eat and remain alive. God's ultimate plan *includes* the destruction of it. Why? Simply because He will create a new one, but this one will be burned to nothing and will pass away completely (cf. 1 John 2:17), since it has been fully corrupted.

The idea that we should go without so that future generations will have, is patently ridiculous. It is nothing more than a slow form of global suicide. While people today die from lack of food, due either because certain areas of earth are off limits for farming, or because certain species of animals cannot be harmed, we smugly sit back and announce, *"At least future generations will have this land to farm and those animals to eat, however, it would be better if everyone becomes vegan!"* It makes absolutely no sense, but anytime Satan is able to attempt upturn God's plan with his (Satan's) own, then we have a problem.

This is what the environmental agencies – and not just those of *our* government – have accomplished because they have given into the voice of those who speak not for God, but for Satan. They do this without knowing it, and certainly, their motives seem on the surface, to be altruistic. Nonetheless, the result is labeling what God has given humanity to use (not abuse) *off limits*. God Himself has indicated that we are to use the earth and its resources for ourselves. This is why the earth is here.

We have become so afraid of using it up, that we have put unbelievable restrictions on using many things at all. The actions based on these restrictions have done nothing to alleviate famine, starvation, disease and even fuel prices.

Being Good Stewards Does Not Mean Not Using
While Christians *must* be good stewards of everything that God has provided, we must *never* take man – who is the highest facet of God's Creation – and put him on the bottom. We must never allow animals or plants to displace man from the position that God Himself placed him in.

Global warming has and continues to be a hot topic (no pun intended). It is one of those areas which strikes fear in people because the experts tell us that humans are responsible for it. So what do we do? We are told to use fewer products that are said to add to the problem of global warming. In truth though, there is not a whole lot we can do about global warming.

A statement on the Greenpeace website states *"Global warming is the most urgent environmental crisis of our time, and we have the solutions — we just lack political will. That's why we're demanding U.S. climate leadership on the world stage, working with business to implement solutions, and exposing the dirty secrets of corporate polluters like Exxon."*[2]

Global Warming...On Mars

Global warming is not a problem that seems to have only affected earth. Some scientists in Canada believe that Mars is experiencing global warming. It would be impossible to blame this on human beings on earth.[3]

There are problems with our world and our environment. As those called Christians, we are to subdue it and use it. We are also to be good stewards of it. This does *not* mean placing anything above man by attempting to conserve it for the next generation. It is more than indecent to allow people living on the earth today to die because a species that they could be eating, is protected. This is how man's value becomes far less than that of animals. That animal then has displaced man and has actually superseded his value. This is wrong. There *must* be a balance.

People for the Ethical Treatment of Animals (PETA) has its own agenda. They would like everyone to become vegetarian. On their website are statements made by various celebrities, endorsing the vegetarian lifestyle. Statements by Paul McCartney, Pamela Anderson, Alec Baldwin and others extol the virtues of swearing off meat forever. McCartney states *"If anyone wants to save the planet, all they have to do is stop eating meat..."*[4] So really, the solution to saving the planet is just that easy, according to one former Beatle.

Please do not misunderstand. Animals should be protected from *abuse* and *mistreatment*. Their lives need to be protected because they are generally unable to protect themselves, once they become domesticated, or caught by humans. Even in the wild, animals are becoming endangered primarily because of illegal hunting and trapping.

What Will Be Will Be
There are often two extremes within society. Many people today have a laissez-faire attitude in which things are allowed to simply happen. Folks who think like this do not fend for anyone else's rights, much less an animal's. The other extreme is the attitude that says "I will do anything I want, when I want!" Neither of these attitudes is productive at all, and instead of helping society, it winds up hurting.

I recall while living in an area of the country which was experiencing a particularly bad period of drought. The city had to make some hard decisions regarding the use of water. One of those decisions included prohibiting residents from watering their lawns and gardens any time they wanted to do so. Instead, a schedule was created and odd numbered homes would water one day, while even number homes watered the next. People were allowed to water three days a week. No one was allowed to fill their swimming pool without permission. Water conservation in other areas was strongly encouraged and other limitations were placed on the public.

Watching a news program one evening after these changes had been instated, the news reporter was asking the average "man on the street" what he thought about the new rules. The person responding looked like he was already out for bear, and when he responded, his words mirrored that demeanor. "The city can tell me what to do with my front yard, but if I want to, I can turn my hose on full force and aim it down a hole in my backyard and they can't say anything about it!" or words to that effect.

If his response wasn't sad, it would have been funny. Instead of working *with* the city government to conserve water, he had the attitude that said "I do what I want and I do not care how my actions affect other people." Obviously, this type of bearing is not one which aids or benefits society.

OPEC is Simply Crude

Crude oil is obviously a big problem in the world and what makes it a problem at all is the fact that one conglomerate called OPEC controls the flow of oil to most of the world. The United States has become much more dependent upon getting its oil from OPEC due to the fact that over the last few decades, fewer and fewer companies are allowed to drill for oil either in the soil of the U.S., or offshore from the U.S. What makes matters worse is when you have the Exxon Valdez oil spill of 1989, in which just under 11 million gallons of oil spilled from the Valdez into the sea at Prudhoe Bay. This amount of oil eventually covered an area of water that measured 11,000 square miles. Unfortunately, while no spill is acceptable, this one could have been avoided, as it was found to have been caused by human error.[5]

If we have oil off the shores of the United States that will free our country from the tyranny of foreign nations, then we *need* to drill for it. Every precaution should be undertaken so that sea life is not destroyed, but we should not treat the oil as if it is not there, because by removing it, living creatures *may* be harmed in the sea.

But then someone will argue that the greed by these mammoth companies is what lays the ground work for tragedies like oil spills to occur from the start. Ultimately though, it is the consumer who is at fault because of *their* desires. The companies certainly exist to turn a profit, but they could not do so without help from, and demands of, consumers.

In the end though, if allowed to go unchecked, humanity may well wind up snuffing itself out because of extreme environmental laws that prohibit the use of this resource or that one. In the meantime, the earth then will continue and the animal kingdom will reign supreme in the absence of man. This is not what God intended at all. However, it is clear from the Bible and from the way Satan works, that this has been his (Satan's) plan from the beginning.

Only Cats Will Survive
I'm reminded of specific documentary-type shows which are titled things like "The World After Humans" or something similar. They are interesting to watch, but the message is one in which extreme environmentalists applaud. These types of programs and the vision that they project cause people to *give up* things altogether, as opposed to simply finding a balance. Apparently, according to one program, cats will outlive humans. Yea, for the cats!

Like PETA and Greenpeace, these groups seem to not want to give up until the world stops using any or all resources. This is wrong, yet the sense from these groups is that if people die so that animals can live, that is fine. This is the world's wisdom and it does not come from God, but from our enemy.

Who then is correct, God or Satan? Whose wisdom should be heeded? When it comes to saving the planet, which is more important due to value; the earth or man?

It's a Balancing Act
A balanced system of good stewardship and the proper use of resources can be reached and maintained. This will only be accomplished when people begin to realize that man is the most precious aspect of Creation that God made. It will only be when we understand that true value of humanity that we will then be clear on how to properly use and preserve the resources that God has given us on this planet.

The earth is here for us to *use*. The resources found within it are to make our world society a better place. We will not destroy it. That "pleasure" if you will, is reserved solely for God Himself, who will then create a new heavens and a new earth as detailed in Revelation chapters twenty-one and twenty-two.

---

[1] http://www.goinggreen.com/ 06/07/2009
[2] http://www.greenpeace.org/usa/campaigns 06/06/2009
[3] http://www.canada.com/nationalpost/story.html?id=edae9952-3c3e-47ba-913f-7359a5c7f723&k=0 06/06/2009
[4] http://www.goveg.com/vegetarian101.asp 06/06/2009
[5] http://en.wikipedia.org/wiki/Exxon_Valdez_oil_spill 06/06/2009

Chapter 7

Hell is So Passé

Talk to many people today and if the topic of religion comes up, the subject of hell is usually not that far behind. Most people are not interested in discussing that issue, because it is not a happy subject. It is not one in which people feel secure, or get a sense of God's love for us.

In fact, the concept of hell is seen as just the opposite, causing the question to be asked that if God truly loves humanity, *how* is it possible for Him to send anyone to hell? The shock with which this question is asked belies the difficulty that people have with respect to hell.

Hell Can't Be Real! It's Too Awful!

Not too long ago, a friend contacted me via email. He was really upset as seen from his subject line which read '*Something really troubling – a false teaching.*' Of course I was curious and concerned. This individual had been struggling with Christianity for some time, and the last thing he needed was to have to deal with false teaching.

It turned out that my friend had come up against the doctrine of *eternal* punishment. He believed that this could *not* be connected to God, who said that He loved people. He was very upset over the whole subject of people being eternally punished for their misdeeds, or sin nature. He made a number of comments regarding it like this one, "*What I'm saying is that it is not logical in ANY way, to hold a mortal and finite being, to an IMMORTAL and INFINITE judgment/penalty.*"

Initially, he did not believe it was taught in the Bible at all. I took the time to go through it with him, pointing him to various sections of Scripture so that he would be able to see it for himself. After studying, he wrote back with "*You are right. I researched eternal punishment, and have come to the conclusion that it IS stated as that, in The Bible.*" He continued though with this statement, "*I think previously, I held to a naive notion, because I didn't want to believe it. Having come to realize this,* **I can no longer call myself a Christian**." (Emphasis added)

The problem for him then came to be the punishment that God determined was just for those who routinely lived in sin, following the dictates of their sin nature, and ultimately for those who died in that sin, without ever coming to Christ for the salvation that only He offers. We spent a good deal of time going back and forth and I know it was very difficult for him. I even sent him some books which I hoped would help him see his way through this doctrine; a complicated issue to be sure.

The furthest point we were able to get to is that he was still having difficulty with the fact that people, as *finite* beings, were being held to an eternal (or infinite) punishment. He considered that to be extremely unfair and dictatorial by God, even making God a "monster." For God, who is supposed to love with an endless love, this was something he found exceedingly difficult to accept. It made absolutely no sense to him and he literally was completely put off by it.

Doctrine of Election Can't Be Real! It's Too Awful!
This also tied in with the concept of predestination, or more accurately, *election* (since predestination is something that is applies to Christians for the work they will accomplish on behalf of Christ *after* becoming saved). He did not understand election either, but in truth, who really can fully grasp it? This is a very difficult nut to crack so to speak. On one hand, people are responsible for their actions and on the other hand, God chooses who will receive salvation. Of course, there is the Arminian version which teaches that God looked down the path of future history before anything was made and finding those who would be amenable to receiving salvation, marked them for it.

I have recently checked in with him and his attitude remains resolute. In no way does he believe that God would allow people to be tormented forever in hell. His words, "*...as a human being, who can see and understand the human perspective, I would not worship any being, who forsakes my fellow man. That is not a god worthy of my worship.*"

The difficulty of course is that he tragically understands very little of the Bible, yet, obviously believes he has a real handle on things. He continued by saying, "*A God who creates mortals (and CONTINUES creating them!), and sends them to an infinite torment, is an ego-centered monster, far more evil than any man could ever be.*"

In other parts of his communication with me, he states he understands sovereignty and believes that God is sovereign. He also indicates that he believes he understands what free will is as well. However, when push comes to shove, he also appears to hold free will in a much *higher* position than God's sovereignty.

God Held Hostage

Like many who make this error, they wind up holding God hostage to man's *supposed* free will. This is really an untenable position, for it presupposes that man knows far greater than God, and is far more equipped to *love* than is God. All it really proves though is that man is incapable of fully comprehending God's sovereign position over all that He has created. It also proves that man is just as egocentric as he has always been.

The other important aspect here is that God *sends no one* to hell. People *choose* it. To be consistent then, because man has free will, he can and does decide for, or against God. To choose against God means to choose the same path that Satan has chosen which ends in the Lake of Fire. This is not really all that difficult to grasp, *unless* one places man above God. By placing man above God, God's views and opinions become far less important than man's views. Man then becomes the most important aspect of everything God has ever done or will do. In essence then, salvation is the epitome of all that God does. Everything is seen to come back to that point. There is nothing higher or more sacred than salvation.

Unfortunately, this is not what is actually taught in Scripture. While salvation is extremely important, make no doubt, it is *not* the most important thing God has ever accomplished. In point of fact, there is something that is much more far-reaching than even salvation. That something is *His glory*. To view salvation as the highest goal God has ever set in motion is nothing more than a *man-centered theology*.

The highest goal of God is to ensure that everything He created glorifies Him. Salvation, which is arguably one of the most important projects that God ever undertook, without doubt brings God tremendous glory. Yet, everything He does brings Him glory. The Creation brought Him glory at one point and will again. There is nothing that will not bow the knee to God, offering Him the glory that is rightly due Him.

God should be glorified for His:

- **Holiness**
    - **Psalms 99:9** *Exalt the LORD our God, and worship at his holy hill; for the LORD our God is holy.*
    - **Revelation 15:4** *Who shall not fear thee, O Lord, and glorify thy name? For thou only art holy: for all nations shall come and worship before thee; for thy judgments are made manifest.*
- **Mercy and truth**
    - **Psalms 115:1** *Not unto us, O LORD, not unto us, but unto thy name gives glory, for thy mercy, and for thy truth's sake.*
    - **Romans 15:9** *And that the Gentiles might glorify God for his mercy; as it is written, for this cause I will confess to thee among the Gentiles, and sing unto thy name.*
- **Judgments**
    - **Isaiah 25:3** *Therefore shall the strong people glorify thee, the city of the terrible nations shall fear thee.*
    - **Ezekiel 28:22** *And say, Thus saith the Lord GOD; Behold, I am against thee, O Zidon; and I will be glorified in the midst of thee: and they shall know that I am the LORD, when I shall have executed judgments in her, and shall be sanctified in her.*
    - **Revelation 14:7** *Saying with a loud voice, Fear God, and give glory to him; for the hour of his judgment is come: and worship him that made heaven, and earth, and the sea, and the fountains of waters.*

The above are merely a few areas in which God deserves our praise for His glory. There are many other areas in which He is owed our praise and gratitude. The concept of praising Him for His judgments may seem a bit odd, however, this speaks of His justice as well as His mercy. Without Christ we are judged and rendered unable to enter into a personal relationship with Him. With Christ, our sin is judged at Calvary, allowing us to enter into a personal relationship with Him. Without His judgments, there would be no salvation.

Trying to thoroughly understand what the Bible teaches is difficult, but it should always come back to God's absolute sovereignty? If you not do begin there, you are going to be way off course.

The Trinity Is Easy to Comprehend?
How many of us can truly comprehend the Trinity? Some argue because it is too confusing, it cannot be of God because God is not the Author of confusion. This is not even *close* to being a worthwhile argument. The fact that God is *infinite* would be more than enough to suggest that there are things about Him we – *as finite beings* – will *never* comprehend, because they are beyond our comprehension. Because we cannot understand or fully comprehend the doctrine of the Trinity is not a legitimate reason to deny its truth.

Getting back to the doctrine of eternal punishment, the only question that needs to be asked and answered is whether or not the Bible teaches such a doctrine. Is hell a literal place? Is it a place where souls of dead unbelievers will be place? Is it a place of eternal torment?

All Those Questions
In the course of His short ministry, Jesus spoke on a number of topics. He spoke a good deal on God's kingdom. He talked about the leaven of the Pharisees. He dealt with and detailed events that would occur at the end of this age, which would usher in the next. He taught about salvation and claimed that the only way to find true salvation was in Him. For those who failed to discover that narrow road which leads to life eternal, there was only one path left for them. That alternative path is the wide road that leads to destruction and according to Jesus, many would find it (cf. Matthew 7:13). This wide road, leading to destruction is one of the ways that Jesus referred to hell. While Jesus

It is All for His Glory

Man's POV

For many, everything culminates in the cross. To them, this is the highest goal that God ever put into motion.

For others, while salvation is the most important thing that God ever completed for man, it is not seen as the highest goal for all that He did, or will do.

God's overarching purpose is NOT found in salvation.

God's POV

For God, the highest goal He has established is that all things will glorify Himself. This means that every aspect of all that God created will praise Him. All will bow the knew, those who are saved and those who are not saved.

Everything about God should be praised. Salvation is without doubt one of the most remarkable things that God ever accomplished for humanity. It brings Him glory, but it is not the only thing that brings Him glory.

God's overarching purpose IS found in His glorification.

spoke of many things, teaching on numerous doctrines, hell is a topic that He spoke about the most.

Hell is NOT the Final Stop

But we need to stop here for a moment, because the idea of hell, while clearly taught in the Bible, is actually not the *final* resting place for the unsaved. That place is called the Lake of Fire. In fact, there are a number of places that are taught and discussed in the Bible that are described as places of torment, with the final place of eternal torment being the Lake of Fire.

In the twentieth chapter of Revelation, we read of both hell and the Lake of Fire. We first read of the demise of Satan, the Antichrist and the False Prophet, *"and the devil who had deceived them was thrown into the lake of fire and sulfur where the beast and the false prophet were, and they will be tormented day and night forever and ever,"* (Revelation 20: 10). Here it is clear that Satan will join the two individuals who participated in helping him in his attempts to take over the world and overthrow Christ. The text is plain enough that these three will be tormented day and night, *forever and ever*.

Hell is a Holding Cell

But what about hell? We learn more of hell in the next section, *"Then I saw a great white throne and him who was seated on it. From his presence earth and sky fled away, and no place was found for them. And I saw the dead, great and small, standing before the throne, and books were opened. Then another book was opened, which is the book of life. And the dead were judged by what was written in the books, according to what they had done. And the sea gave up the dead who were in it, Death and Hades gave up the dead who were in them, and they were judged, each one of them, according to what they had done. Then Death and Hades were thrown into the lake of fire. This is the second death, the lake of fire. And if anyone's name was not found written in the book of life, he was thrown into the lake of fire,"* (Revelation 20:11-15).

Notice that we are privy to a scene in which a great white throne exists and we turn our attention to "him" who was seated on it. The *"him"* here can only be referring to Jesus. Notice the reaction of the elements everywhere; *"from his presence earth and sky fled away, and no place was found for them."* Even the earth and sky are afraid of Christ's majesty and perfection.

We then notice that all of the dead; those who were considered great by earth's standards and those who were considered small were all standing before Him, and before His throne. This is one tremendously large multitude of individuals, and it appears that they are awaiting their judgment.

The Books
They do not have to wait long because the books were there, and were already opened. Then another book is said to be open, which is the book of life. So the first set of books contains everything that each individual has done in this life; things that *they* might consider good and things that *they* might not consider to be good. Ultimately though, it does not matter at this point what these individual people believe about their works since the prophet Isaiah tells us that all of anything we consider to be *good* is nothing but filthy rags as far as God is concerned (cf. Isaiah 64:4-9).

It is easy to fool people into thinking that we are truly altruistic, but it is impossible to fool God. Since people cannot see within us, they are not privy to all that transpires within. God, on the other hand, sees beneath the outer shell into the heart of the person and judges based on that.

Now notice as we move along in these specific verses, we get to the part which says *"Death and Hades gave up the dead who were in them, and they were judged..."* (Revelation 20:13). So both Death and Hades (which is another term for *hell*) give up the dead that are contained within them. They are given up in order to be judged.

Death and Hades End Up Here

But then notice what occurs with both Death and Hades. Verse fourteen of chapter twenty explains that both Death and Hades *"were thrown into the Lake of Fire."* This then, from this same verse, is the second death. This becomes the ultimate place where unsaved of all generations, nationalities and cultures will be placed, once their judgment is complete.

As if to emphasize and drive the point home, verse fifteen states tersely, *"if anyone's name was not found written in the book of life, he was thrown into the lake of fire."*

So in the end, it is the *Lake of Fire* which becomes the eternal home of those who were unable to find – for one reason or another – the narrow way which leads to life eternal.

Hell is a temporary residence, as it were. It is a place where the unsaved dead go until they are resurrected *for judgment* prior to being unceremoniously thrown into the Lake of Fire. The judgment here is not to *determine* whether or not they are going there. It is to show each individual *why* they are going there. There are no second chances at this point, as they have been given a lifetime of chances in this life. There are no reprieves. This is where the sentence is imposed *and* carried out on each individual who died without Christ.

Some of the Scriptures we can see explain more about hell. In effect, hell is:

- a place of absolute awareness (cf. Luke 16:23,24)
- a place of palpable darkness (cf. Matthew 8:12)
- a place of eternal separation from loved ones (cf. Luke 13:28)
- a place where there is absolutely no chance or hope of release (cf. Matthew 25:46).
- a place where memory itself adds to and becomes part of the torment (cf. Luke 16:27,28).

- a devouring fire (cf. Isaiah 33:14)
- an everlasting fire (cf. Matthew 25:41)
- a fire that is never quenched (cf. Mark 9:43)
- a place where the worm does not die and the fire is not quenched (cf. Mark 9:46)
- a place of outer darkness (Matthew 8:12)
- a place of weeping and gnashing (Matthew 8:12)

God is Not Only Loving

So if hell is all of this and more, but still only a temporary place until each person is thrown into the Lake of Fire, the question that must still be answered is *how could a loving God throw anyone into hell for all eternity?*

It is a fair question and one that deserves an answer. The difficulty becomes that some do not *like* the answer and have a hard time wrapping their brain around it. Because of that, they prefer to reject the doctrine as being man-made. They believe because *they themselves* love (they think), yet imperfectly, how much more should God Himself love people?

In other words, these people who have a difficulty with the concept of a loving God and eternal hell believe that they love others. Because they love others, they would not want to see those others be tossed into a place like hell or the Lake of Fire for all eternity. If they – though they are human – are *that* concerned about other human beings, then how much more should *God* be concerned about human beings, since He is said to love *perfectly*?

The answer is not an easy one to appreciate. The failure to grasp the answer has more to do with man's inability to not only love as *God* loves, but to superimpose upon His character the character of fallen man. *"The ultimate proof of the seriousness of sin and the justice of everlasting punishment is provided by the cross of Christ."*[1]

God is absolute *love*. There is no doubt of this. The most famous verse in Scripture – John 3:16 – alone bears this out: *"For God so loved the world that He gave His only begotten Son that whoever believes on Him should not perish, but have everlasting life."* We understand to an extent that God's love *caused* Him to want to do something for fallen humanity. It was His love that produced the plan of salvation, which resulted in the horrible, painful death of His Son. It was due to the atonement of Jesus Christ, on Calvary's cross that salvation was made available to humanity at all. While we can still not fully comprehend that, we *can* appreciate the fact that it was love in action; and a tremendous love at that.

Now though, we are expected to believe that this very same God of love, who gave up His only Son in order that salvation would be made available to whosoever will, also created hell and the Lake of Fire. The Lake of Fire is the final place of every individual who ends up separated from God and it is in this place that they will be tormented day and night, forever.

Lake of Fire Created for Satan, Originally

However, the original reason for which hell and the Lake of Fire were created, should be understood. Was it for man? The Scripture says otherwise. Both Jude and Peter speak of hell as being a place where some fallen angels have been chained, reserved specifically for judgment (cf. 2 Peter 2:4; Jude 6). These places were *originally* created for the devil and his angels (cf. Matthew 25:41). Why? Because they chose to rebel against God Almighty, Maker of Heaven and Earth. Satan himself sinned when pride was found within him (cf. Isaiah 14) and after sinning, he convinced one-third of the existing angels to follow him in his rebellion.

God then created this eternal fire, or Lake of Fire for these beings. However, since that time man has been created and Satan found a way to cause Adam and Eve to rebel against God as well. Because of this, the sin nature came into existence and transferred from one individual to the next through physical birth. Since according to Paul, all have sinned and fallen short of the glory of God (cf. Romans 3:23), like Satan, all deserve to be tossed into the Lake of Fire as Satan eventually will be.

However, *unlike* the devil and his angels, man is given opportunities to repent and turn to God for salvation. This is something that will never be offered to Satan, or his horde of demonic hosts. They fell with God in plain view. They saw God for who He was/is, and yet rebelled against Him anyway. They literally lived in the light of His countenance and perfection, but did not consider that to be enough. For them, their sin is unpardonable.

Only Man Was Created in God's Image
The Bible nowhere teaches that either Satan or any of the angels were created in God's image. This special privilege was reserved only for man. None of the creatures God created prior to Adam were endowed with this special gift. It was Adam only, who became the height and glory of God's Creation.

Because man was made in God's image, he is redeemable and though man sinned (and *continues* to sin), God made a way for man to come back to God. Throughout each person's life here on earth, God gives them as many chances to repent and receive His salvation that they need. Only those who receive Christ's salvation are admitted into heaven. Only those who recognize their fallen state and their inability to help themselves get back to the place where man was prior to the fall, are given admission to God's eternal abode.

So if man gets all the opportunities he needs in this life to receive salvation, yet continues in unbelief and sin, the question to ask is *not* whether or not a loving God can toss anyone into the Lake of Fire. The question that needs asking is *whose* fault is it when each individual person refuses to acknowledge his need for salvation? Whose fault is it because people reject God's salvation?

Whose Fault Is It?

The answer in every case is: *man's*. It is man's fault for not finding God. It is man's fault for not turning to God in repentance. It is man's fault for going in the footsteps of Satan and his angels to begin with and it continues to be man's fault for allowing his own arrogance and lack of humility to keep him from finding God any way that he can.

If God created the Lake of Fire originally for the devil and his angels and man follows in that same path, is not God just in allowing man the same fate? The answer is *absolutely*. He is not less loving because He allows people to choose the Lake of Fire over Him. He longs for them to come to Him, but no one is forced to do so.

Is it right to blame God for the actions of individual men who refuse to repent and even refuse to see any *need* to repent? How is that just on man's part? God has created the way back to Him. He has provided the impetus and He raises up people to call others to come to Him in repentance and in faith. Those who answer that call are blessed. Those who reject that call, walking away from God are cursed. How is this *not* just?

But, say some, while they can understand a need for punishment, eternity is *forever* and it seems as though the punishment is far greater than the crime. Do these people honestly believe that when people die in unbelief, having rejected God throughout their earthly life, that they all of a sudden *stop sinning?* Is this what people believe?

How would it be possible for a person who lived solely for himself in this life, all of a sudden change so that in eternity, he now wanted to (more to the point, was *able to*) live for God? That is an absolute impossibility.

Those who die in sin in this life, *continue* to sin in the *next life*. Simply because their life is over on this planet, does not mean they stop sinning in the afterlife, as if death somehow eliminates an individual's sin nature. Sinning is *who they are* and by default is *what they do*. The Christian, if not for Christ, would do the same.

It is only because of salvation that the ability to stop sinning is *implanted* within the Christian, due to the presence of the Holy Spirit and His indwelling power. Though unable to live a perfectly sinless life for the remainder of the time here, the *ability* to *not* give into temptation is *now* part of life. As Christ's character is created within, the Christian can now draw on that character in order to overcome temptation and become more like Christ Himself. This is accomplished through the indwelling power of the Holy Spirit, who also seals the believer unto the day of redemption (cf. Ephesians 4:30).

The Process of Salvation
While salvation begins for everyone at a specific point in their life, it is also a *process*. A number of things happen instantly, and the sealing of the believer by the Holy Spirit is one of them. Another thing that occurs is that each believer's unrighteousness is exchanged for Christ's righteousness. When God the Father looks at me, He does not see my filth, caused by my sin. He sees Christ's righteousness instead, which allows Him to look favorably upon me. This is why Paul can confidently say that *"There is therefore now no condemnation for those who are in Christ Jesus,"* (Romans 8:1).

Because Christ's sacrifice was so perfect, since His life was absolutely sinless, the salvation that comes to each believer includes *His* righteousness. This is why there is absolutely *nothing* I can do to earn my own salvation (cf. Ephesians 2:8-10). Salvation is entirely a gift of God, needing nothing else to make it "work." God does not need or want my *deeds* in order for me to be somehow made worthy to receive salvation, as most cults teach.

Salvation is perfect. It is the required propitiation that allows God to grant eternal life to those who trust in Jesus' atonement. There is nothing else that will grant salvation. There is nothing that can be *added* to salvation. It is already perfect in itself.

The question that really should not be asked is "How can a loving God send people to a place of eternal torment?" The question that should really be asked is, "How can even *one* human being reject the only path which exists to gain access to God?" Those who reject it are literally asking to be sent to that place of eternal torment, because they have done exactly what Satan and his angels have done. The consequences of such action in all fairness, should be the same. In the end, it *is* the same.

Nonetheless, most still ask the question which they believe hinges upon God's loving kindness; *how could a loving God toss people into hell for all eternity?* First of all, people who ask that question do so because they are unable to appreciate

- the tremendous sacrifice of Christ as the atonement for sin
- how desperately wicked sin is and how much God hates it
- that they are actually emphasizing man's perspective, not God's

To Excuse is Divine
To many of us, sin is often a laughing matter. We find excuses for our sin and believe that because God is said to be so loving, that He will excuse the "little sins." Of course the difficulty with that is that there is *no* sin which can be described as *little*. All sin is a form of rebellion and as such, it is *all* directed against God and His sovereignty as well as His holiness.

God's justice cannot permit sin to go unpunished. He must punish sin. He cannot simply set it aside and ignore or forget it, unless there is something that *pays* for the damage it causes. Because Adam and Eve sinned, they were immediately judged guilty by God, in spite of their excuses as to what provoked their sin. A choice was made by God during the pronouncement of His judgment. A curse had come upon the entire Creation, and man himself now had to deal with a sin nature that was always and forever diametrically opposed to God and His will. In spite of this, God had also created something that would relieve man of his debt; the debt created by His sin. This is exactly what salvation entails and it is what God hinted at in Genesis 3, when He told the Tempter that though he will bruise the heel of the woman's seed, her seed will bruise the Tempter's head. This is a fatal blow (cf. Genesis 3:15).

Victory Over Death!
Though Christ actually *died* on the cross, in spite of what some religions and cults teach, His was not a death that kept Him from rising again. The perfection of His Person and His life brought Him forth from the grave in glorious splendor, with an incorruptible body. The Tempter on the other hand, though he did not die on the cross physically, was, nevertheless, destroyed even so, an event which will take place in the future, as appointed by God in eternity past.

Because of sin's curse, the debt which sin created was extremely high and continuing to grow. In order to pay it off, as it were, something of infinite value was required. That something was the very life of the Sinless God, who became Man, yet retained His full deity, using it only when it coincided with the Father's will.

As Christ lived His earthly life out for the 33 years or so that He walked this planet, He did so as an example of how man was supposed to live. This is the reason He referred to God as His Father. This is the reason He referred to God as His God. This is the reason He said He came not to do His own will, but to do the Father's. This is the reason He did everything the way He did it. It was to show humanity how man was supposed to live before God.

People argue about whether or not Jesus was actually God, and they point to all the times He said things like I have just stated, and appeared to be in a subservient position to God the Father. It was solely for the purpose of being a living example to humanity, so that we would *know* how to live before God, and so that we would not be able to claim ignorance at knowing how to live. Christ came to be an example and as that example, He took it to the furthest point available; innocently dying for the guilty.

People who ask how a loving God could send people to an eternal hell are only concerned about themselves and their viewpoint. In fact, as with my friend that I quoted from earlier in this chapter, these people seem overly confident that they have the perfect reason to disbelieve in the doctrine of hell. They believe they know more than God and everyone who does not agree with them is wrong.

All of this though leads us to ask this very important question beautifully worded by Donnelly, *"What sort of God would treat good and evil in the same way? If God could look at sin and say, 'It doesn't matter; it is of no real concern to me; forget about it, for I will; welcome to my heaven', he would be God no longer."*[2]

God is Holy, Just and Fair

If God is loving, He is also just, holy and *fair*. In fact, there is no one who is more fair than God is when dealing with the wrongs that have been perpetrated in our world. He is so fair in dealing with these problems that He alone is the only one who can say *"Vengeance is mine...I will repay,"* (cf. Deuteronomy 32:35; Psalm 94:1; Romans 12:19; Hebrews 10:30).

How could God who expects people to live righteous lives (and has provided the one way for that to be accomplished), turn around and admit those who have never taken advantage of that salvation, so that they might enter in with those who have taken advantage of it? In receiving salvation, my righteousness is removed and replaced with Christ's perfect and complete righteousness.

This is the process we refer to as *justification* because it is through this process that I am able to stand justified before God. While the Old Testament stressed the need for it, the sacrifices of animals could not provide it. This is why the animal sacrifices were required to be done over and over.

Conversely, Christ died once and that took care of the sin problem because His perfection which allowed Him to pay the full debt with plenty left over. As it states, *"For Christ also suffered once for sins, the righteous for the unrighteous, that he might bring us to God, being put to death in the flesh but made alive in the spirit,"* (1 Peter 3:18; cf. Hebrews 9:26; 1 John 3:5; Isaiah 53:11).

Perfect Atonement for Imperfect Humanity
Because Christ's atonement was perfect, that one act of death, and shedding of blood dealt with sin. All that was left was for each person to – by faith – receive that gift of eternal life that is available through Christ. Our faith is in Him and His finished work on our behalf. Sadly, for whatever reason, those who die, having continually rejected this salvation in the here and now, enter eternity having to rely on their own "righteousness." We know from what the Bible tells us that our righteousness is *"as filthy rags"* (cf. Isaiah 64:6; as far as God is concerned. There is nothing righteous about it. It rises like a stench to His nostrils. We are all guilty of sin (cf. Romans 3:23). We cannot stand before Him and argue that we did not sin like "that murderer over there." It makes absolutely no difference sin all sin is lawlessness; a form of rebellion (cf. 1 John 3:4; 1 John 5:17; Romans 4:15).

"Unbelievers use hell to accuse God of a lack of love, a failure to be merciful. However, the truth is that there is mercy. For in Christ 'God demonstrates His own love toward us, in that while we were yet sinners, Christ died for us' (Rom. 5:8)."[3] We cannot be excused when we place blame on God's shoulders. The blame lies directly with us and yet God has provided the remedy. He is not at fault when we sin, He is not at fault when we refuse to receive His salvation, and there is no fault

found within Him when because of this, each sinner goes to the place of eternal torment. It is the self-centered, "all about me" individual who believes that God is held accountable because people are born who end up in hell.

Not too long ago, I pulled up to someone whose taillight on their vehicle was burned out. I rolled my window down to let them know. Having come from an eastern state, I was all too familiar with the safety checks that were done on automobiles every year to determine whether or not they would pass or fail and be allowed on the road again. Taillights that did not work were an easy fix.

I leaned out of the window slightly and yelled a bit (to be heard) to the driver that their passenger side rear taillight was burned out, and they might want to fix it. The driver looked at me, stone-faced, raised his hand, and then held up his middle finger. I wasn't sure if I was supposed to admire this ability he possessed to manipulate his finger in such a way or not, but you can imagine that I was taken aback by this! Here I was offering this individual some information about his car that I would certainly appreciate knowing, but to this, instead of appreciation, I was on the receiving end of his rancor. I was too dumbfounded to do anything except merely stare at him for a second or two before the light turned green and we both went our way.

Certainly, a burned out taillight is not a big deal, unless you routinely use your blinker as a courtesy to other drivers, and like it when others do the same. In this case, it was nothing more than a piece of information that I had hoped the driver would appreciate knowing, in order to be able to fix it before he got pulled over and received a ticket. He chose to view my courtesy as an insult to him and responded as if I had mistreated him.

Salvation is an issue which needs to be dealt with by each person. To ignore it is to ignore the outcome of this life. To ignore it means not taking seriously the fact that death for everyone will occur and then we all face God.

"The traditional doctrine of hell now bears the mark of odium theologium – a doctrine retained only by the most stalwart defenders of conservative theology, Catholic and Protestant. Its defenders are seemingly few. The doctrine is routinely dismissed as an embarrassing artifact from an ancient age – a reminder of Christianity's rejected worldview."[4]

Hell is Just an Allegory

The author of the above quote – Al Mohler – points out that Origen offered the *"first major challenge to the traditional doctrine of hell."*[5] This is really no surprise, since he is known also as "Mr. Allegorical" by any number of historians. His proclivity to allegorize Scripture has done major damage to the plain text of the Bible, adding, or subtracting from God's Word seemingly at will.

Except for those who believe that the Bible clearly teaches the doctrine of eternal torment and damnation, there exists within society and Christendom two major beliefs:

1. universalism
2. annihilationism

Universalism is the belief that *all* people will be saved. It matters not how "bad" someone is according to society's view. The only thing that matters is that God is so loving that His love preempts allowing any individual to go to a place we would label *hell*. It is unthinkable and therefore rejected, because it is said to be diametrically opposed to God's loving character.

While at least some universalists agree that the concept is not taught in Scripture, they hold to this belief due to their deep revulsion regarding an endless punishment for those who end up there, due to decisions made in this life. These people believe that God will not rest until everyone, including Satan and those who fell with him, are brought back into fellowship with Him.

"Rejecting all thought of an endless hell for some is prompted partly, to be sure, by direct compassion for one's fellow humans, but mainly by the thought that inflicting eternal punishment is unworthy of God, since it would negate his love."[6] This particular quote sounds like something my friend could have easily said, of whom I referred to near the beginning of this chapter.

The Universal Approach
Universalism then presupposes two things, 1) they and they alone understand the love of God as revealed through His Word. Anything else makes a mockery of it; and 2) since all will be saved eventually, evangelism is not all that important. This is, of course, in spite of the fact that Christ issued the command to preach to all nations (the Great Commission). The main task of the Christian is one in which social and economic conditions are noted and dealt with throughout the world.

Annihilationism is the belief that not all will inherit heaven for their eternal home. Those who do not are destroyed. By being destroyed, they are annihilated, becoming as if they were never born.

Both of these theological errors stem from a re-imagining of God's love. The biblical definition of God's love is either changed or replaced with a definition that is more suited to those who are either proponents of universalism or annihilationism. *"In Scripture, God's love appears framed by three realities. The first is his ownership of, and dominion over, all that he has made – that is* his universal lordship. He is always God on the throne and in control. *Second is* his holiness, *the quality whereby he requires virtue and purity of us, recoils from our vices and rebellion against him, visits the vicious with just judgment for what they have done, and vindicates himself by establishing righteousness in his world. The third reality is* everybody's actual sinfulness *and constant failure to match God's standards and obey his Word. It is within this framework that the divine way of acting – which the Old Testament usually calls goodness and loving-kindness (covenant love) and the New Testament calls* agapē *and* charis *(grace) – finds expression."*[7]

It is clear from the writings of universalists that they view God's love differently than the biblical teaching. In the Bible, we see God's love as working to *restore* humanity to the place of relationship with God. This is made possible through the redemptive work of Christ, which culminated on Calvary's cross. This restorative nature of God's love is either received, or rejected by those on earth. If received, they are at once restored into fellowship with Him. If rejected, they are not restored. If once leaving this earth, they have died without ever receiving God's love in order to be restored into fellowship with Him, the chances of being restored to Him are all in the past.

God's Love is Just...Uneven
For the universalist then, God's love is not seen as something that restores people to Him. His love is seen as something that progressively deals with, and allows people to come back into fellowship with Him. It will start in this life, but may not culminate until the individual moves into eternity through the door of death. In this case then, those who immediately go to hell, are enabled to continue to be on the receiving end of God's love. This love, over time, ultimately brings the person back into His fellowship. At such time, they can then move out of hell, as they have been made fit for heaven.

Of course this concept, negates the terminal illness humanity has, and which the Bible refers to as *sin*. Sin is not only terminal, but it is something that God loathes. It is doubtful that words do justice in our attempts to explain just how much God hates sin, and is repelled by it. Those who die in their sin become exceedingly sinful. They continue to sin in eternity. They slowly and painfully languish over all of eternity, becoming more and more like their sin.

It is also clear that for the universalist, and others like them, they place a much greater emphasis on the concept of *love* and *free will*. They view God as being unable to do much more than simply try to influence us to see it His way. Because of this, it is said He will not (nor can!) barge into our lives to get us to do things we do not necessarily want to do. In essence then, His hands are tied and He becomes *limited* because of our free will.

No Such Thing as True Free Will

The actual truth of the matter though is that no human since Adam and Eve (and later Jesus), actually has a true free will. In the Garden of Eden, Adam and Eve were essentially *predisposed toward God*. They had the perfect ability to choose either *for* or *against* God. Because they ultimately used their free will to choose against Him, they then became slaves to a constant desire to rebel against Him. Adam and Eve sinned and fell because of that sin. What was created within them was the sin nature, and what was taken *from* them was actual free will, in the truest sense; something that we do not have today.

What every human being since then has, is not the same free will that Adam and Eve had. Our free will – if it can be called that – is one in which our desires are largely set *against* God's lordship. Everything about us – our desires, our thoughts, our motivations, our words, our actions – all work against God. This is not free will. Due to the fall, we have become prisoners of our will, which is not *free* in the slightest.

It is only through Christ that we have an *opportunity* to get back into relationship with Him. This is made possible through our faith in the atonement of Christ on Calvary's cross. His atonement and our faith in that atonement, free us from the bondage to sin. Our will is now loosed (though still not perfectly), which allows us to make decisions when temptation approaches. Will we, or will we not follow God? Will we say 'no' to temptation, or will we follow its dictates?

Those who believe that free will plays such an important role in our life are in error. People arrive at these erroneous conclusions based solely on a reliance on *rational thought*. *"When rational persuasion is the ace, inbred irrationality trumps it. Bodily addictions such as pill-popping and heroin-shooting can, we know, defy all attempts at therapy; is there any reason to suppose that the habit of sin will be easier to talk its addicts out of, even when our loving God is doing the talking?"*[8]

Does Our Free Will Control God?
People who believe that somehow our free will is so strong that we can control it, turning it to the direction we wish it to take us, are living in a world of fantasy. This is not where humanity is, with respect to any type of free will. Our free will stopped being truly free when Adam and Eve fell. Every other person born after that suffers with that same fallen will (except Christ); as if each individual had done exactly what Adam and Eve had done, and reaped the consequences of their actions. How could it be otherwise? The human race came ultimately from Adam and Eve *after* they fell; after they rebelled against God and were cursed because of it. Any offspring they would have would carry that same fallen sin nature and imprisoned will.

Those who give heed to the notion that they are in control and have the ability to decide for or against God, seem unaware of the truth of the matter. They prefer their own rational thoughts, to the unchanging truth of God's Word.

Annihilationism espouses that anyone who dies without Christ, will be destroyed into *non-existence*. While this belief has been around for some time, it stems largely from a misunderstanding of the use of words like "destruction" "destroyed" "second death" and merely "death" itself.

In all of these, the Bible never means to go completely out of existence. Death in the biblical sense is always a form of separation. We see that with our first parents, Adam and Eve, in Genesis 3. After they had sinned, God announced that what He had warned them before they fell would now come to pass. He had told them ahead of time that if they ate of the tree of forbidden fruit, they would die. Once they had committed that act, they *did* die. They died spiritually, which was a break in fellowship with God. They were no longer able to walk with God in the Garden of Eden, while He instructed them about Creation. Now, they became segregated from Him, as evidenced by the fact that they were kicked out of the garden and not allowed re-entrance.

They also began to die physically. In pronouncing judgment, God told Adam that it would be by the sweat of his brow (something Adam had not yet experienced), that the earth would give him food. In other words, he would have to work for it. This very act of working, while tiring and even sometimes exhausting, would actually prolong his life by keeping him healthy. It would stave off the effects of physical death that his body immediately began to experience.

Once Adam reached the point of actual death, his spirit left his body, and his body continued to die, or decay. This decaying process took time, but it was all part of the process of death. His spirit, having left his body, was alive, and continued to think and understood that he was a person, or a living soul. Death is always separation from one thing to another.

Extinction

Annihilationism is *not* taught in Scripture *anywhere*, that this author could find. Neither Christ nor the apostles taught this concept. They warned of an eternal punishment for the wicked; those who continued to reject the gospel of Jesus Christ. Whether they change the meaning of the words directly related to death, or whether they modify the meaning of words like eternal, the fact remains that they are changing what God so clearly teaches.

Douglas Moo addresses this. *"Definitive conclusions about the meaning of these words in each case are not easy to attain. But this much can be said: The words need not mean 'destruction' in the sense of 'extinction.' In fact, leaving aside for the moment judgment texts, none of the key terms usually has this meaning in the Old and New Testaments. Rather, they usually refer to the situation of a person or object that has lost the essence of its nature or function..."*[9]

Hell is an unfortunate fact of eternity. The tragedy though is that it *can* be avoided, but often, is not. Too many people believe that hell is either not a real place, or it is certainly not as bad as some imagine it to be. After all, a God who perfectly loves humanity, would not send people to hell. Of course the truth is that He does not, as mentioned. Each person decides for themselves where they will spend an eternity.

Hell is just as much of a fact, as is heaven. Both are eternal. Both are real. Both will have people in them. Both are accessible by all. Those who choose to receive the salvation offered by Christ bypass hell, because He paid the price. Those who choose to reject the salvation provided by God have only their own works and their so-called righteousness to rely on. Neither will save them and in fact, both will condemn them, since in their case, both their works and their righteousness will be compared to Christ's, who is *the* standard.

"What will you say when you stand before God? He will remind you that you were warned, more than once. But you would not listen. You 'trampled the Son of God underfoot' and 'insulted the Spirit of grace' (Heb. 10:29). If you refuse to believe in Christ, if you will not receive Him as your savior, you will be damned and you will deserve to be."[10]

As much as we might hate and be repelled by the doctrine of hell, it is real according to the Bible. This is why many evangelists throughout the centuries have used descriptions of hell to often scare their listeners into taking God seriously. Our finite minds are unable to picture the full brutality of hell. Neither can we fully comprehend the concept of eternity. The Bible teaches that hell is both of these things, and this reality, by those imprisoned there, is something that they will be unable to shrink from experiencing.

God Always Has a Way Out

But the opposite of hell is heaven; eternal death or eternal life. God loves but without punishing sin, He would be completely *unjust*. In His love, He has provided a way back to Him, through the salvation offered by Jesus Christ. Those who reject Him, reject *life*. Those who reject Him have nothing to look forward to except an eternity of His anger; anger directed at *them* for the sin they have committed, for the sin they represent, and for the glory that initially diminished God's glory.

---

[1] Edward Donnelly, *Heaven and Hell* (Carlisle: Banner of Trust, 2005), 27
[2] Ibid, 29
[3] Ibid, 29
[4] Christopher W. Morgan, Robert A. Peterson, Gen Ed, *Hell Under Fire* (Grand Rapids: Zondervan 2004), 16
[5] Ibid, 17
[6] Ibid, 172
[7] Ibid, 190
[8] Ibid, 193
[9] Ibid, 203
[10] Ibid, 31

Chapter 8

The Days of Noah Again

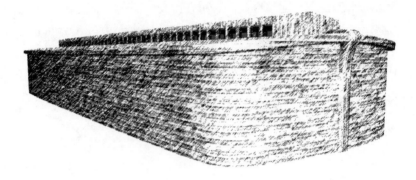

"Just as it was in the days of Noah, so will it be in the days of the Son of Man." (Luke 17:26)

Luke is the only gospel in the New Testament in which Jesus makes the statement shown above. In the seventeenth chapter of Luke, Jesus is teaching and speaks of a number of things prior to making the noted statement regarding Noah. In His teaching, Jesus discusses things like increased faith, and the inevitability of sin, but "woe" to the one through whom sin is introduced to others. He also takes the time during His journey to Jerusalem to stop and heal ten lepers.

Those Annoying Pharisees

As usual, the Pharisees were not far behind Jesus, always looking for an opportunity to fault Him and find ways to condemn Him. In this particular instance, the Pharisees have asked Him a question regarding the kingdom of God and *when* it would arrive. Jesus answers it simply by stating, *"The kingdom of God is not coming with signs to be observed, nor will they say, 'Look, here it is!' or 'There!' for behold, the kingdom of God is in the midst of you,"* (Luke 17:20).

Though He seemed on one hand to be denying a physical return (as some teach), it is apparent that Jesus was speaking of a kingdom that was *based* in, and started with, a spiritual renewal, something which was ultimately and only found in Jesus and His kingdom. At the same time though, He was not in any way negating the truth of His future, personal return (as proven in the verses immediately following), since the two concepts are not in any way mutually exclusive. In truth, when Jesus said that the kingdom of God was in the midst of the Pharisees, He was obviously speaking of Himself, because He was standing among them. There was no fanfare. He was just there, and from all outward appearances, did not appear to be anything special.

Jesus continues with His teaching about the future coming of His kingdom, comparing the circumstances surrounding its arrival with the time of Noah (as well as Sodom and Gomorrah). This is very important for us to grasp. Luke 17:26 He says, *"Just as it was in the days of Noah, so will it be in the days of the Son of Man. They were eating and drinking and marrying and being given in marriage, until the day when Noah entered the ark, and the flood came and destroyed them all."* Here Jesus is clearly stating that His physical return will have circumstances that existed in the world very similar to that of Noah's day.

Likewise, beginning in verse 28, Jesus compares His future physical return to the time of Lot, when Sodom and Gomorrah were physically and literally destroyed. The circumstances surrounding the destruction first of the world with the global flood and then with Sodom and

Gomorrah are intriguing. Jesus specifically chose these two situations for us. Certainly, at least part of the reason He chose these two is due to the exclusiveness of the judgment that God sent. In each case, many lives were lost. Beyond this, livestock was lost, homes were destroyed and in effect, there was nothing that remained after each of these judgments were poured out from God's hand.

Both of these events described by Jesus physically occurred, as will His return. Just as the flood waters took everyone outside the Ark by surprise, in spite of the fact that Noah had preached to them for roughly 120 years, Jesus' own return will take everyone who is not watching by surprise. Just as the destruction literally rained down upon the twin cities of Sodom and Gomorrah took everyone by surprise, so will Jesus' return affect the world in like manner. The only individuals who were spared were Lot, his wife and their two daughters. However, even they did not get much warning at all. In effect, the destruction of those twin cities took everyone by surprise.

Scoffing at the Truth
We are increasingly seeing this type of reaction to the preaching of Christ's Second Coming today, with much more regularity. People are more often quick to disagree with the idea that the world will see Jesus return *physically*. Many within Christendom prefer to think of His return in *spiritual* terms, because it simply sounds too unbelievable to the average person that Jesus is actually going to come back to earth and set up His kingdom.

This entire subject, which is part of the overarching prophetic discourse which Scripture provides related to the end of the age, has become something that people either downplay, deny or ignore altogether. From a biblical viewpoint and all that is said about this day and age, it makes sense that this would be the attitude of many. It should be noted as well that it has only been within the last few decades that the denial of the physical return of Jesus has come to the fore within Christian circles.

Here are Jesus' words regarding Noah's world, "*They were eating and drinking and marrying and being given in marriage*" (Luke 17:27), and His comment related to Lot's day, "*were eating and drinking, buying and selling, planting and building*" (Luke 17:28). What He is obviously saying is that things were going on normally, at least as normally as can be expected in spite of the fact that people had become extremely perverted. Apart from their perversions, they still did the normal, everyday things that most people do in their lives on a daily basis. People ate and drank, were married, gave their children away in marriage, they bought and sold goods and planted crops and built buildings. These are all very normal things for people to do and it does not matter whether they are labeled evil or good by others. These are things that all people participate in.

Is There More for Us?

However, is there more here that Jesus wants us to see? Is there something that He hints at (by choosing these two specific situations) that He wants us to be aware of, as the time of His return approaches? There are a number of biblical scholars who believe that this is the case. They believe that in order to truly understand what Jesus is saying here, we need to do some investigating into the biblical text. This will allow us to understand just exactly what the conditions were like in either of these situations.

In spite of the fact that these people did things which all would consider to be normal aspects of day to day living, it is clear that the people during both Noah's day and Lot's, were *exceedingly wicked*. They participated in things that the Bible is clearly set against, but does not give us a great amount of detail on. Even though during Noah's day and age, we are told that "*every intention of the thoughts of [man's] heart was only evil continually*" (Genesis 6:5b), they continued to do things that are considered normal by our standards.

Is Jesus trying to tell us something more than things were simply done normally, when He says "as it was in the days of Noah"? Chuck Missler in *Alien Encounters* brings some interesting information to the forefront of today's discussions, regarding Christ's reference to the days of Noah. It may serve us a good deal to find out what we can find out about the people who lived during those days. This in turn may provide us with information about how evil they were, which will provide us with a picture of how evil people *will become* just prior to His Second Coming to earth.

Missler looks specifically at the Genesis 6 passage and finds those verses to be interesting to say the least. He believes that these bizarre circumstances which existed prior to the global flood offer insight for us today.

The Nephilim
Prior to learning that all men did and thought evil all day long, we discover that an interesting situation existed on the face of the earth. Genesis 6:1-4 states this, *"When man began to multiply on the face of the land and daughters were born to them, the sons of God saw that the daughters of man were attractive. And they took as their wives any they chose. Then the LORD said, 'My Spirit shall not abide in man forever, for he is flesh: his days shall be 120 years.' The Nephilim were on the earth in those days, and also afterward, when the sons of God came in to the daughters of man and they bore children to them. These were the mighty men who were of old, the men of renown."*

There are a number of things in this passage which require investigation to determine their meaning. We see the phrase "sons of God" as well as the word "Nephilim." We notice that the sons of God found the daughters of man to be beautiful and because of that, decided to take them for wives. In fact, they took "any they chose" to be wives. We get this sense that it was not necessarily a mutual feeling, or that the women in question might not have had much of a say at all.

So who are the sons of God and who are the Nephilim? Missler believes that the sons of God referenced here are angels. He is not the only one. Numerous biblical scholars like Fruchtenbaum and Stephen Quayle believe this as well (Quayle's book *Giants* goes into quite some detail, based on his 30 plus years of studying the subject). Missler references the fact that when the Septuagint version of the Torah came into existence, having been translated from the Hebrew, the *sons of God* expression was translated *angels*.

If these sons of God beings were actually angels, this may help us understand the comments made by both Jude and Peter in their New Testament letters. Apparently, at least some fallen angels had done something so horrendous that God found it necessary to lock them up since that time.

Some Angels Did Something Really Bad
Jude 6 makes this comment about these angels, "*And the angels who did not stay within their own position of authority, but left their proper dwelling, he has kept in eternal chains under gloomy darkness until the judgment of the great day.*" Something obviously occurred involving some angels, which required God to keep them chained. Now it *cannot* be that the crime of these angels was following Satan in his rebellion. If that was the case, then *all* angels would have been locked up. Only some of the angels committed a particular sin that God determined to be so heinous, that it required chaining them up. What was it? It very well could have been that some angels found a way to procreate with human women, thereby creating a hybrid race of beings which are called *Nephilim* in Hebrew. Missler and others have stated that this Hebrew word "*literally means 'the fallen ones' (from the verb* nephal, *to fall). In the Septuagint translation, the term used was...gigantes, or 'earth-born' They are also called...*Hag Gibborim, *the 'mighty ones,' or 'hero,' or 'chief-man'.*"[1]

This is certainly interesting and if this is so, then it would provide the reason for God needing to chain these creatures. Missler continues, "*apparently these unnatural offspring, the Nephilim, were monstrous and they have been memorialized in the legends and myths of every an-*

cient culture on the planet Earth...the Nephilim also seem to be echoed in the legendary Greek demigods. Throughout Greek mythology we find that intercourse between the gods and women yielded half-god, half-man Titans, demigods, or heroes which were partly terrestrial and partly celestial."[2]

Of course it must be asked, aside from the horrendous nature of sin with which these beings perpetrated (if that was indeed the case), why would the offspring of such beings be such an affront to God?

Missler points out that the Bible clearly notes that out of all who lived on the planet, only Noah was considered "perfect" in his generations. In other words, apparently Noah's lineage had not been *"tarnished by this intrusion of the fallen angels."*[3]

Corrupting the Human Race

There is really only one reason why Satan would have some of the angels who fell with him attempt to *change* the human line, creating hybrid creatures who were part-human and part-angelic. If he could successfully corrupt the human line, then it would be *impossible* for a Messiah to be born through that line. Satan knew from Genesis 3 what was in store for him. He knew that one day, a Savior/Messiah would be born through the woman ("the woman's seed"; cf. Genesis 3). He also knew that this seed of the woman would deliver a fatal blow to him, while at the same time obtain salvation for the fallen human race. If he could somehow negatively alter the human race, it would be impossible for a Savior/Messiah to be born. No Savior/Messiah? No salvation, and no fatal blow to Satan.

It is also very interesting that by the time Israel arrives at the borders of the land of Canaan as recorded in the book of Numbers, there were giants living in that land. Somehow then, even though God destroyed the earth with a global flood, these Nephilim (the offspring of the fallen angel-human female union), were able to get things going again. Their presence in the Promised Land was enough to scare most of the

Israelites. In fact, the account of this as recorded in Numbers chapters 13 and 14 uses the same term; *Nephilim*.

This should not be considered strange, because Genesis 6:4 states, *"Nephilim were on the earth in those days, **and also afterward**,"* (emphasis added). It appears then that the Nephilim were on the earth during Noah's day and also appeared again after that time. It is not unusual then that we find them in the Promised Land; the very land God had set aside for His nation Israel! It is not surprising at all if Satan was behind this unholy union in the first place during Noah's time, that he would somehow manage to have some of these Nephilim waiting for Israel when they arrived at the borders of their new home.

The Nephilim Appear AGAIN!
We know that according to Numbers 13 and 14, out of the 12 spies who went in and came out of Canaan, ten spies reported a completely negative situation, emphasizing no faith in God whatsoever. Only Joshua and Caleb believed that God would give them the victory and encouraged the people to go in and take what God had set apart for them.

Many years later, David dealt with one of these individuals who quite possibly was a Nephilim himself; *Goliath*. This Philistine warrior, as it turns out, was the smallest of his four brothers (cf. 1 Samuel 17)! The Philistines should have been destroyed by the invading Israelites when Joshua led them into the land, but they failed to obey God. Because of that, the Philistines became a thorn in the side to Israel and remained such for many generations.

So how did these Nephilim manage to survive the global flood of Noah's day? Missler believes that *"The Nephilim, the unnatural offspring, are not eligible for resurrection. The bodies of the Nephilim, of course, were drowned in the Flood. What happened to their spirits? Could they be the demons of the New Testament?"*[4]

Missler believes that the demons of the New Testament were/are actually the disembodied spirits of the Nephilim from the Old Testament. While the fallen angels who cohabitated with human women were chained in darkness until their still future judgment, their hybrid offspring became disembodied when their bodies were killed in the Flood.

Even though the *Book of Enoch* is not a divinely inspired work, nonetheless, it contains information about these fallen angels and their Nephilim offspring, which serves to potentially bring more of this mystery into the open. It would seem that these fallen angels were originally called *Watchers* in the *Book of Enoch*. It was the Watchers who, according to the *Book of Enoch* were instructed by God to watch over the earth. Apparently, 200 of these Watchers began to lust after human women. They fell into sin when they followed their lust and entered into marital relationships with these women. The Nephilim offspring was the result. The *Book of Enoch* indicates that as the offspring (Nephilim) died, they became the evil spirits, who are destined to roam the earth. Their job, if you will, is to harass, oppress and corrupt humanity. Another book which bears testimony to this is the *Book of Jubilees*, which as Missler states confirms that the beings referred to as demons in the New Testament, are the same "*disembodied spirits of the Nephilim.*"[5]

The Bible is Far-Fetched; UFOs Are Real

So does this have anything at all to do with society today? It sounds far-fetched to be speaking of angels somehow entering into physical relations with human women. It also sounds far-fetched to talk of offspring, which are essentially hybrids of this union. The Nephilim that resulted from that are described as giants. While of course not all biblical scholars agree on this, it is plausible. While it cannot be proven beyond doubt, certainly historical archaeology may have something to offer us in the way of testimony. We will get to that in a moment.

First, let's answer the question, what do giants, fallen angels and hybrid offspring have to do with us today? Well, if Jesus was intimating that the days of Noah was very much normal by today's standards (regarding people marrying and giving in marriage and buying and selling, as well as building), yet there was something so evil about people that God opted to destroy them, it would seem as though these Nephilim may well have something to do with today's society.

Missler goes into the area of UFOlogy, which as many are aware, is the science of studying paranormal activity as related to other-worldly beings. We know that incidents of UFO sightings and even abductions have increased over the past number of decades, certainly since the 1950s. What was once considered to be spoken of in secret, by individuals who might have been labeled crazy, is now routinely discussed by people from all walks of life today.

In a previous chapter in this book, we discussed the beliefs held by many within the New Age movement, as related to some future great evacuation of what will be millions of people. We learned that the idea of aliens from other planets coming to earth for the sole purpose of evacuating millions of people (who are keeping the planet's evolutionary agenda from occurring), is not only not far-fetched, but commonly believed by many adherents of New Age tenets. This is not an absurd belief for them. It is something that is very easy for them to believe. It can happen and according to many, it will happen.

Could these the spirits of these dead Nephilim be behind this, working jointly with the fallen angels who fell with Satan? Could they be attempting to achieve the same goal? What have they to lose if they fail? They are already destined for the Lake of Fire. If they succeed, then they will be far better off. What better way to deceive the human race by pretending to be aliens from other worlds who have come here in alarm to save the planet from itself and the people on it who are holding it back.

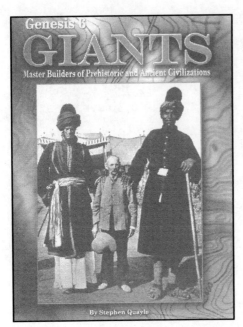

Giants Exist

Stephen Quayle in his book, *Giants*, also has some interesting things to point out. This book is really an in-depth study of Genesis 6. He has studied this area for over 30 years and has come to some intriguing conclusions. He notes that archaeology (and even accidental discovery), has uncovered human skeletons which tower over people today. His book includes a chart of skeletons which have been found over the centuries, some as tall as 36 feet! That is extremely difficult to believe, isn't it? However, this is what the Carthaginians are believed to have located sometime during 200 – 600BC. Other skeletons unearthed in various parts of France are smaller. A 25-foot skeleton was reportedly discovered in 1613, near the castle of Chaumont. Apparently, according to Stephen, nearly the entire skeleton was found intact. Others 23-feet tall and 19-feet tall were found in other parts of France. Quayle also reports that a human skeleton that was roughly 15-feet tall was found in Turkey in the late 1950s. This one was located in the Euphrates valley while roads were being constructed. It seems that other giants were also found there.[6] The front cover of Quayle's book shows two extremely tall men on either side of what is likely a normally tall man. As can be seen, the two men on each side literally tower over the man in the middle (above)! Quayle has numerous real photos of actual giants on his website that are certainly worth viewing, and can be seen at www.stevequayle.com.

These sizes are difficult to imagine, and even more difficult to believe. Yet, many of these are well documented. It is also very interesting that we see that people are becoming taller and taller and have been growing for decades. During the 1950s, it was the norm for a man to be about 5' 7" tall, or slightly higher. Many of the leading men of Hollywood were *under* this height.

Difficult to Believe

The tallest man living today (that we know of), is Bao Xishun, who stands 7 feet, 9 inches tall. The tallest living woman in the world is Chao Defens, who stands 7 feet, 7 inches tall. It is common knowledge that Robert Wadlow, who died in the 1940s, stood just over 8 feet, 11 inches tall! This is an incredible height, yet Goliath would have been taller by at least seven inches!

One has to wonder *why*, within the last eight or so decades, people have started getting taller again. Basketball players during the 50s and 60s were not as extraordinarily tall as they are today. In fact, no one blinks an eye when they find another basketball player someplace in the world who is close to 8 feet tall, or taller. It is becoming common to see men who reach this height. What is *not* being suggested is that these people are Nephilim. What is being stated is that some of the same circumstances which existed during the days of Noah, seems to exist during our day as well. One also wonders what *will* occur after the Church has been Raptured off the planet and the "he who restrains" is "taken out of the way"?

Do these giants have anything to do with the world's state now? Does the rise in UFO sightings and abductions play any part? Is this all part of a massive delusion that is turning people away from God, and focusing on the paranormal?

There are many things occurring within society that are nearly taken for granted today, yet were hardly believed at all not that long ago. The changes in attitude toward the Bible, and God are *telling*. While people are finding it more and more difficult to believe in a place of eternal torment, strangely enough, they seem to have little difficulty believing in UFOs and aliens who say they have come to help us. Like

Missler says though, why are their messages to us always involving something of a religious nature? Why are they not sharing their medical knowledge that one would think they would have if they are that much further advanced than we are on this planet?

Does God Lie, or Does Satan?
All of this, coupled with the disbelief in Jesus' physical return, the Rapture, the fact that Israel will rise again, and many more biblically-related events is certainly something to wonder about. Either what God has stated in His Word is true, or it is not. The things that are occurring today seem to be much more than just coincidence. The denial of biblical truths that have long been held is definitely reminiscent of Paul's warning that in the last days, many would fall away, giving heed to seducing spirits who want nothing more than to pull them away from the truth of God's Word. We see this happening in the Church and it has been happening for some time.

It is also important though to understand that those who believe and preach that Jesus' kingdom is spiritual *only*, have a great deal to prove from Scripture. To deny something is one thing. To prove it another. The question then becomes, *can* they prove it? This author certainly does not believe their assertions have been proven, yet they continue on, resolutely espousing their belief that Jesus already returned spiritually in A.D. 70. Since that has occurred, then there is no physical return that we need to be concerned about, they say. They cavalierly announce that no one needs to be worried by any supposed "Tribulation" or "Great Tribulation." It already happened, so why worry?! If that is the case, we *should* be able to look back at history and see the absolute worst time of human history occurring during the A.D. 70 events.

During A.D. 70 Roman siege in which Jerusalem and the Temple were both destroyed, and the Jewish people scattered, the *tribulation* experienced at that time should have been so great that the world would have experienced *nothing* like it and will never again. Is there any way to measure that level of persecution? We believe there is, and we also believe that determining that level of persecution will allow us to see whether or not there has been anything worse either before or afterwards. If it turns out that this period in history was *not,* in fact the greatest/worst tribulation the world has ever experienced, then the A.D. 70 period *cannot* logically be the Tribulation/Great Tribulation that Jesus spoke of, which was to occur on this planet.

The "World" as Jesus Meant It
It must also be determined what Jesus meant by His use of the word "world" as He described how bad things would get. Was He simply speaking of local events that would be largely limited to Jerusalem and the Temple and the then-known world, or was He describing events in which the *entire* planet would become embroiled?

Many of the individuals who support the notion that the Tribulation/Great Tribulation has *already* occurred make the mistake of thinking that the age we are presently living in is being ruled and guided by Christ, as *King*. They conveniently believe that since He is ruling from His Father's throne in heaven now, that this fulfills the covenant God made with David that someone future would sit on his throne *forever*. We need to distinguish between Christ's physical rule, His spiritual rule and the sovereignty of God in general. To confuse these things is to come to a wrong conclusion, doing a great deal of damage to the integrity of the Scriptural text.

It is clear from many parts of Scripture that God literally rules over the earth. This cannot be denied, in spite of the way things may *appear* to those of us living here. Either God is in complete control, or He is not at all in control. It cannot be both ways. He is either far above all earthly powers (including the "free will" of human beings), or He is held hostage by those powers. We believe the former is applicable to God. In His absolute sovereignty and power, He controls all events occurring on this planet. He oversees them, allows them or directly plans, implements, and brings them to fruition. God cannot be *partly-sovereign*, because that is *not* sovereignty.

One of my favorite passages in found in Psalm 2, which states *"Why do the nations rage and the peoples plot in vain? The kings of the earth set themselves, and the rulers take counsel together, against the LORD and against his Anointed, saying, 'Let us burst their bonds apart and cast away their cords from us.' He who sits in the heavens laughs; the Lord holds them in derision. Then he will speak to them in his wrath, and terrify them in his fury, saying, 'As for me, I have set my King on Zion, my holy hill.'*

"I will tell of the decree: The LORD said to me, 'You are my Son; today I have begotten you. Ask of me, and I will make the nations your heritage, and the ends of the earth your possession. You shall break them with a rod of iron and dash them in pieces like a potter's vessel.'

"Now therefore, O kings, be wise; be warned, O rulers of the earth. Serve the LORD with fear, and rejoice with trembling. Kiss the Son, lest he be angry, and you perish in the way, for his wrath is quickly kindled. Blessed are all who take refuge in him."

God's Sovereignty Not in Question
The Psalm above, without equivocation, addresses God's sovereignty, and too many of us in this day and age, *downplay* it. God is here seen as THE absolute Sovereign Ruler over all the earth. There is no question that God laughs at those who try to plot against Him, as the Antichrist will do toward the end of the Tribulation/Great Tribulation period of seven years.

Even in this Psalm, God's patience is evident, as He takes a "let's wait and see" approach by warning those who would deign to think that they could possibly take God on and overcome Him. A hint of sarcasm can also be seen in His words *"Now therefore, O kings, show discernment; Take warning, O judges of the earth"* in verse 10. God is giving the leaders of this world a chance to bend the knee *volitionally*, or they will be forced to do so.

God's patience is incredible, yet how often is it truly appreciated? He owes us nothing, yet we act as if *we are the ones* who have been wronged. So desperate are we to evade His sovereignty and rule that we come together to gang up on Him, as if our puny, finite ability can take anything from God, or overcome Him. His sovereignty over all His creation is very clear from His Word. So, when Jesus speaks of His own kingdom, certainly in one respect, He *is* ruling through His Bride, the Church, however He is *not* ruling from the actual throne of David.

Davidic Covenant

The reader may recall that God promised David that someone from his line would rule from his throne forever (cf. 2 Samuel 7; Psalm 78:67-72; Psalm 89:3-4; Psalm 132). Some argue that Christ *is* ruling now, from heaven, seated on His Father's throne. While this is true, His Father's throne is *not* David's physical throne, and it should never be confused with it. If these were interchangeable, then we could rightly say that David himself ruled from God the Father's throne, at God's right hand. We know this is not the case at all. How then can we interchange David's physical throne with God the Father's heavenly throne when the ruler is Jesus? While some interchange these two thrones as if they *are* the very same, it is the truth of Scripture that separates these two thrones.

If we consider a number of important facts concerning David's throne and God's covenant with him, we will have a greater understanding of the nature of Christ's reign. We know that David had a *real*, *physical* throne in which he ruled over a peculiar people; the *Israelites*. This throne and rule then, was of a *political* nature as was Solomon's, who became the king after David, his father. Israel was a real place, given to the Israelites by God Himself. *"Solomon's throne was a literal, political throne; therefore the ultimate fulfillment through Messiah will also be literal and political (as well as spiritual). God reiterated the future fulfillment of the Davidic Covenant to David in Psalm 89. God swore in an oath to David that his lineage would continue forever and that David would have a descendant ruling above the kings of the earth (Ps. 89:3-4, 27-29, 33-37)."*[7]

The only way to get from a physical, literal, political throne to one that is *all* and *only* spiritual, is to *allegorize* the text. There is, however, no need to allegorize anything. In fact, there is nothing in the original Davidic covenant (or any reference to it afterwards) that prompts us to interpret it in an allegorical way. God's covenant to David announced a literal, physical reign of David's descendant. Since David's throne began as literal *and* physical, there is nothing in all of Scripture that would support this very same throne *becoming* a spiritual-only throne. Yet, this truth is unfortunately not enough to keep people from making this grievous mistake.

Though some theologians today express doubts about the eternal nature of the covenant, it seems plain that the prophets saw a literal fulfillment of this covenant in their future. *"They reiterated the promises of the future fulfillment amid Israel's sin and apostasy (suggesting the unconditional nature of the covenant)."*[8]

God's Repeats What He Said
It would appear that there is a reiteration of this conviction through many of the prophets, including Isaiah 11:4-5, Jeremiah 33:15-17, Ezekiel 37:24-28, Hosea 3:4-5, Amos 9:11 and Zechariah 14:4, 9. The clarity with which Scripture heralds this truth regarding the fact of Christ's physical Messianic rule cannot be denied. The only way it *can* be denied is when the texts of these prophets is seen in figurative language. In that case of course, the interpreter then becomes the subjective determiner of meaning, denying the absolute truth which God reveals and replacing it with man-made substance, which is no substance at all.

In truth, Jesus' time as physical King over a physical kingdom (which will incorporate the entire world), is not yet, but it *is* coming. It will come to fruition during a time in which He *will* rule the globe and will do so with a rod of iron, as we are told in Revelation 2:27. He will literally crush all revolt and rebellion as He sets up His physical kingdom in Jerusalem, Israel, and from there He will take control of all things on this earth; every *nation*, every *person* and every *dominion* and *power*.

Daniel's Statue Comes to a Crushing End
If we look back at the book of Daniel, it is not complicated to understand what the statue of Daniel 2 reveals. The reason is due to the fact that the text itself tells us. We know that the first kingdom is Nebuchadnezzar's own Babylonian Empire, which is represented by the head of the statue. The next empire to come along is the Medo-Persian Empire. This empire will give way to Alexander the Great and his Hellenistic Empire. The fourth empire highlighted in the passage was the Roman Empire that took over their part of the world. All of this is described for us in Daniel 2:31-45, by Daniel himself, as he relays this information to Nebuchadnezzar.

What is interesting here is that no one doubts that these kingdoms were *actual*, *physical* kingdoms. It is impossible to deny this, since the Bible itself provides the interpretation and then future history (from Daniel's perspective) became reality, just as Daniel outlined. In fact, there are critics of the Bible who find this section to be so accurate that they claim it came *after* these events, written by an imposter who chose the name Daniel. This of course has been disproven, but to the critics, that truth does not matter.

So what we have are four *physical* kingdoms, with each newly established kingdom replacing the previous one. Finally we get to the fourth kingdom, which appears to have "died" only to be raised again. Many have thought this was a reference to the *leader* of this empire, but in all probability, it is likely the reference to the *type* of empire which existed at this time, of which none like it had existed before; *imperialism*. This is brought out by Arnold G. Fruchtenbaum in *Footsteps of the Messiah*, quite clearly.

Imperialism By Any Other Name

The Roman government was essentially an imperialistic form of government, and history bears this out. While there was one ruling Caesar at a time, governors and tetrarchs were chosen to rule and oversee individual areas of the Roman Empire. In this way, the Roman government had one main capitol which was where Caesar's seat of power was located and that was normally in Rome. However, as the Roman armies fought against and took over other areas of the world, increasing the size of their empire, it became too large for one individual to rule over all of it. Governors and tetrarchs would become Caesar's eyes and ears in the various parts of the Roman Empire. This is *imperialism* because Rome sent their *own* people to rule over various newly acquired territories, as opposed to using people from within that territory, as had been done during Nehemiah's day for instance (cf. Nehemiah 1ff), and in all previous empires.

This is what separated the Roman Empire and way of governing from the previous empires that it *swallowed* up. Previous to Rome, this type of government was not used. Again, for more on this, the reader is encouraged to obtain a copy of Dr. Arnold G. Fruchtenbaum's book *The Footsteps of the Messiah*, in which he goes into some great detail.

Nonetheless, these individual empires were *real*. They were *physical* and *actual* and they had real *human* rulers who sat on real, physical thrones. Probably the most interesting thing about this vision, was the fact that after the last empire "rises" again and fills the entire world, a Stone hits the feet of the statue, completely destroying it, leaving nothing but dust in its wake. The exact wording is "*And in the days of those kings the God of heaven will set up a kingdom that shall never be destroyed, nor shall the kingdom be left to another people. It shall break in pieces all these kingdoms and bring them to an end, and it shall stand forever, just as you saw that a stone was cut from a mountain by no human hand, and that it broke in pieces the iron, the bronze, the clay, the silver, and the gold,"* (Daniel 2:44-45a).

Only God's Kingdom Is Just Spiritual?
So while many prefer to see the kingdom of God as being *only* spiritual, the text of Daniel without doubt indicates otherwise. None of this contradicts what Christ teaches in Luke 17 though, because He essentially states that there will be no sign preparing anyone for the instantaneous return of Christ. Immediately after His coming, He will set up His kingdom. When will this occur? It will happen at the end of the Great Tribulation, when the Antichrist's power is at its zenith. This Antichrist will believe himself to be indestructible and will have already set himself up as god to be worshipped by humanity (referred to as the *Abomination of Desolation* by Christ, in the Olivet Discourse). This is detailed for us in Revelation 19, starting with verse 20, when the Beast (another name for the Antichrist), decides to make war against Christ and those who followed Him. With the breath of His mouth, the fire that proceeds from Christ destroys the Antichrist upon His return to earth, in preparation to setting up of His kingdom.

The Abomination of Desolation spoken about by Christ in Matthew 24 is an event which was something that Jewish people living during that time would have known of, which is why the comment "*let the reader understand*" is made in verse 15. This historical event is understood to be the event in which Antiochus Epiphanes perpetrated when he walked into the existing Jewish Temple of his time, into the Holy of Holies and slaughtered a pig on the altar. He then sprinkled blood from the pig around the Holy of Holies and also set up a statue of Zeus there as well. This act of course, defiled the Temple, effectively stopping the sacrifices. This gave rise to the Maccabbean Revolt of which the name Judas, the Hammer became known.

The Abomination of Desolation Revisited
Christ referred to this event because He was stating that this same

type of an event would take place in the future (from His POV), when the final ruling tyrant would waltz into the Holy of Holies. He would then proceed to declare himself to be god and would demand that he be worshipped. This would again defile the Temple and even though this same individual had made the original covenant with Israel, they would then wake up to the realization that they had been completely duped.

There is no place in history that this author could find where this event occurred, since the time of Christ. It would appear then, that this event still needs to take place. Christ is effectively stating that the Antichrist in Matthew 24, will be the one to do this, but only after he has gained control of the *entire* world. Christ's reference to the world is just that; a reference to the *entire globe*. In other words, Jesus is saying that this Antichrist, the last Satanically-led and inspired leader to attempt assault to God's throne and sovereign rule, will at one point have the entire earth under his control. Christ is *not* speaking here of the *then-known* world, or some localized empire, but of an empire that will control all of the planet.

No World Rulers...Yet
Since Christ's time, there has not yet been one individual who has ruled the entire globe. It is something that *will* occur, but has *not*. The Abomination of Desolation is something that this coming ruler will perpetrate against the Jewish people and something which will obviously occur after they have once again started up the sacrificial system. While the Israelites of today seem in many ways to be preparing to for this time of a renewed sacrificial system, the actual sacrificial system has not yet begun and it cannot begin until at least part of the Temple is rebuilt on the Temple Mount. The one thing that keeps the Temple from being rebuilt in any form is the presence of the Dome of the Rock Mosque, which many believe sits where the Temple sat.

The Bible shows that the sacrifices will begin again. We know this because the future Antichrist's act of defiling the Temple by declaring that he is god, will cause the *cessation* of the sacrifices. In order for them to be stopped, they will have to have been *started*. This has not occurred, so we can safely say that this is all yet future. Certainly though, the time seems to be drawing closer and closer.

As remains clear from the many interpretations of Scripture that appear on the landscape of Church history through today, many Christians view the words of Christ in Matthew 24 as pointing to the destruction of Jerusalem and the Temple which took place in A.D. 70. They believe this historical event is the fulfillment of what Christ was teaching His disciples. These people state that Christ *did* return then - *spiritually* - and He returned in *judgment* on the nation of Israel because of their rejection of their Messiah. They also point to Nero or some other Roman ruler as the Antichrist.

Christ Speaks Plainly
The problem of course, is that Christ seemed to be plainly speaking of the *end of the age*. Which age is that? It seems clear enough that He is speaking of the end of *man's* age, which will segue into the age of the Messiah upon His return. According to Fruchtenbaum, the rabbis of old essentially spoke of two ages, this age and the age to come. The *age to come* is always thought to be the *age of the Messiah*. The Messiah has not physically returned yet, therefore we are still in *this age*; *the age of man*.

We have also not witnessed any type of Abomination of Desolation. Though many attempt numerous Scriptural gymnastics to show a connection with the A.D. 70 events, it is a stretch to be sure to tie anything that occurred during this time with the Abomination of Desolation. Some deny that the Antiochus debacle was actually the original event of which Christ referred. Yet, this event by Antiochus stands out as the abomination of abominations from history past. To be sure, it is to this event that Christ was referring to when He informed His listeners that an event very similar to that would again occur. It is a focal point of past history that will again be replayed on the field of warfare by Antichrist in his attempts to deify himself and be recognized as such by the entire world.

While it is obvious that at least *some* of what Christ prophesied *was* fulfilled in the A.D. 70 events (the destruction of Jerusalem and the Temple), not all of what He referred to did. Christ speaks of the end of the age and of His coming, which will be clearly visible. Because of His coming, *all* the tribes of the earth will mourn. This is a global reference, meaning *all people on the earth.* He is not merely speaking of the twelve tribes of Israel here, in Matthew 24:29-31:

"Immediately after the tribulation of those days the sun will be darkened, and the moon will not give its light, and the stars will fall from heaven, and the powers of the heavens will be shaken. Then will appear in heaven the sign of the Son of Man, and then all the tribes of the earth will mourn, and they will see the Son of Man coming on the clouds of heaven with power and great glory. And he will send out his angels with a loud trumpet call, and they will gather his elect from the four winds, from one end of heaven to the other."

In the above passage, a number of things occur:

1. The sun will be darkened (this is a total blackout)
2. The moon will not give its light
3. Stars will fall from the heaven
4. The powers of heaven will be shaken

"In the Matthew account, Jesus stated that just preceding the sign of the Second Coming of the Messiah, there will be a total blackout of the earth. No light will penetrate to the earth from the sun, the , and the stars (Matthew 24:29). Luke adds that there will be a great amount of perplexity on the earth as both physical and non-physical things are shaken in expectation (Lk. 21:25-26)."[9]

Nature Announces His Return
Dr. Arnold Fruchtenbaum's commentary here points to the fact that

just prior to Christ's return as Messiah, nature itself seems to know what is about to occur. It is a setting much like what might occur before a ballet, symphony, opera, or other concert event. The lights go out in expectation of the main event. After a few moments of expectant anticipation, the lights go on, the curtain rises and the event begins. It is the same with Christ's physical return.

These four events just listed, set the stage for His return and as can be seen from the events themselves, it is not a happy occasion for those who have gathered to fight against Him. Psalm 18:8-16 speak of this return and phrases like "smoke out of his nostrils," and "fire out of His mouth" are descriptions that help us understand the tone and calamity which surrounds His return. He returns to take care of business, right the wrongs, judge the nations and set up His kingdom. He will sit upon the throne of David and will rule the world from Jerusalem, which has always been and always will be God's Holy city.

Dr. Fruchtenbaum says this about His coming, as described for us in Psalm 18, *"At His Second Coming, He will come with the wrath of God (vv. 8-9), riding upon a cherub (v. 10), which will have horse-like features, according to Revelation 19:11. There will be convulsions throughout nature at the Second Coming (vv. 11-15) as the entire world is illuminated by the brightness of His glorious return."*[10]

The Shechinah Glory Sign

Fruchtenbaum also points out that he believes that the "sign" spoken of Matthew 24:30 is referencing the *Shechinah Glory* which was often highlighted in the Old Testament (cf. Numbers 9 and 12, as examples). Think of the event of Christ's Second Coming, and the moments leading up to it. First, there is total darkness over the entire earth. Then the Shechinah Glory literally bursts forth dispelling that darkness. All eyes will turn to the sky as Jesus Christ, Lamb of God, Messiah to Israel, returns to His earth, as Judge, Jury and King.

"As It Was in the Days of Noah"

In the Olivet Discourse in Matthew 24, Mark 13 and Luke 21, Jesus speaks of events which will occur prior to His return. None of the things listed below have occurred in either A.D. 70, or in our present time. This means they are still yet to occur in the future. There is no reason to see these things in terms of allegory, or as figurative language when the literal meaning is obvious.

Signs of His Near Return	*A.D. 70?*	*Today?*
7-year Covenant signed with Israel?	No	No
An Absolute *World* Ruler Yet?	No	No
Abomination of Desolation?	No	No
Final Conflict Led by Antichrist?	No	No
Complete Blackout in Heavens?	No	No
Shechinah Glory Out of Darkness?	No	No
Christ's Physical Return?	No	No
Christ Judged the Nations?	No	No
Christ Ruled from David's Throne?	No	No

What Christ has taught here, referencing the days of Noah, is found in the latter part of the Olivet Discourse (cf. three of the gospels; Matthew, Mark and Luke).

Christ's reference to the days of Noah *precede* all of these events, which lead up to His return. Jesus points out that prior to the worst time on earth, things will be as they were during Noah's time as well as Lot's time. In some ways, things will go on as they have for centuries. However, it is important to determine whether anything was unique about those particular times on earth that may also wind up appearing during the period immediately before the worst tribulation the world will have ever known.

Nope, Just Don't See It
If the reader can find a time in history past where the tribulation per-

petrated against believers has been the most severe ever, there might be the slightest sliver of a case to believe that Christ has indeed returned and the Great Tribulation has already occurred.

The difficulties with this view are many. The Bible clearly shows Jesus' return as *physical* and the *immediate death* of Antichrist with His return. After this, Christ judges the nations and then sets up His physical kingdom on earth. He will then reign for 1,000 years from His 'father' David's throne. Upon the culmination of his reign, **He will then turn over the title deed of earth to the Father**. In order to be able to do this, Christ *must* actually, physically reign over the entire earth first. He must sit on David's throne as Ruler and as Ruler, He will then be able to give to the Father the title deed to earth, having fully wrested it from all powers, principalities and dominions. This is all detailed in the book of Revelation. Christ will have fulfilled the Davidic Covenant, and during this same period, Israel will have her land as a possession forever.

All Glory To God
All things culminate in Christ. In fact, this is where everything has been leading since before the foundations of the earth. Salvation, an intricately woven and supremely important aspect of this overall plan, is not the only or final phase of God's plan. The entire plan was predicated on the idea that God is sovereign and that everything He does should in turn bring glory to Him.

Everything Will Glorify God
In fact, as we look through the entirety of the Bible, we see things that appear at first glance to *not* glorify God, yet out of those things, God brings glory to Himself. Whether it was the fall of Adam and Eve, the evil perpetrated against Joseph by his jealous brothers, the pain and agony which Job experienced, the birth, life, death and resurrection of Jesus Christ, the birth of the Church, the Tribulation/Great Tribulation itself and many, many other events; all bring glory to God in some form or another.

There is nothing that does not, nor will not, glorify God as *the* only wise God. There is no other. All wannabes and pretenders to the throne will be seen for who and what they are, in their attempts to usurp God. He will share His glory with no other. All of that glory stays within the three-fold nature of the Godhead.

God's overall aim is that everything that occurs in this life will bring Him glory. This is and will happen, as so decreed by God Almighty. There is nothing that will not ultimately bring Him glory. Even Satan will glorify God. He will at a specific point in our time, bend the knee to Jesus Christ declaring Him to be above all other gods.

Wrapping It Up
What I have endeavored to do in this book is to introduce the reader to a number of the *major lies that Satan has perpetrated* and continues to perpetrate on the world. To Christians, he would prefer us to believe that there is no Rapture, yet to those outside the Church, he is preparing them to understand the Rapture will occur, with his perspective, not God's.

Satan would like us to believe that God is *not* in control; that His very sovereignty is in question, yet the Bible confirms a completely different understanding. God has *never* lost any aspect of His sovereignty and maintains it still. There has never been a plan B.

Satan would like us Christians to believe that we must tone down our "rhetoric" and come alongside the world. We must stop our condemnation of things that God condemns. We must stop "hating" those who live a different lifestyle. We must love them and for Satan, this means that we remain hidden in the shadows and never come out with God's viewpoint of sin.

Satan: the Greatest Salesman Ever
Satan wants us to buy into the environmental belief that turns things upside down; supplanting man and places animals and plants on a

higher plane. We are not here to use the earth, but are here to *save* the earth for future generations. Never mind that food could be used today, or scientific breakthroughs could be discovered today, if only we were allowed to harvest specific trees or grow more crops in that area of the world, or that one. We must preserve the earth so that people of the future will have it for *their* needs. Forget our needs now. We must stop with our selfish viewpoints and look beyond ourselves to generations that will come after us.

Satan, the accuser of our souls, prefers that we believe that aliens and beings from other planets are here as benevolent missionaries. He wants us to be taken in by their message, their motives, their appearances, even though the messages are routinely of a religious nature. They offer no secret medicinal knowledge which might allow us to eliminate cancer, the common cold, AIDs, or any other diseases that routinely destroy the lives of millions yearly. Their message is very similar to that of the New Age movement's message, which says, at its core, that we are all *divine*. We only need to activate that divinity within us in order to come to the full realization of who we are and what we can accomplish. Though this sounds very much like the situation that existed during the building of the Tower of Babel, since no *physical* tower is being built, there is little danger of it being mistaken for such.

In the end, there is truly nothing new with Satan's scheming. He has always wanted to be greater than God, though he himself is a *created* creature, with powers that were *given* to him by God Himself. He continues to teach that we can be like God. Instead of telling us that God is jealous and therefore does not want us to be like Him, the new twist is that *all is God* therefore, we are already God. Since we are already God, then as we grow in that knowledge, unlocking the secrets found only within the divine, we realize just how much we are able to accomplish (read *create*), and that our own lives are only limited by our lack of knowledge regarding our inherent deity.

Same Old Lies

Satan truly has nothing new to offer humanity, but by the looks of things, he *needs* nothing new. With each new generation of people, he has lied a little bit more, brought more things to bear, and caused what was once seen as weird and strange, to become commonplace.

The tragedy of course, is that in the midst of all of this, people fall into eternity on a daily basis through death, and without Christ. Satan cares not one iota for them and in fact, delights in their eternal demise. He has gained a large foot-hold in many mainline churches, where he has been able to present his lies as truth. He has raised up many ministers who work solely for him; they without realizing it, in many case. Their judgment is still warranted and will come unless they turn from their own life that tries to negate the truth of Christ. Like Judas who knew Christ on one level, but was never renewed in his spirit, these false ministers do not tremble, or fear God in any way, shape or form. They blatantly offer and teach blasphemies that serve Satan, and those who hear them and follow them are no better off than those who espouse their lies.

Satan's Agenda Not So Hidden

Satan has an agenda. That agenda is to dethrone God. His final attempt will be through the Antichrist, a man who will be completely endowed with Satan's attitude, demeanor and power. Together with the False Prophet, these three – *Satan, Antichrist and False Prophet* – will make up the *False Trinity*, that attempts to mirror the true Trinity.

The Counterfeit Trinity

This False Trinity detailed in the book of Revelation, will have its day, but it will not gain the victory. It will gain the very thing that was created for them; the Lake of Fire, which was created for the devil and his angels.

A time is certainly coming on this earth (and is here now), when God's truth will be more and more seen as falsehoods and Satan's falsehoods seen as truth. It is the Christian's obligation to choose whom this day who will be served; Satan or God? It should not at all be a difficult decision to make, yet it is becoming more difficult with each passing day.

God's Will or Satan's?
As Alan Redpath has so very accurately stated in a book of his sermons, compiled by his wife, this thought should be the theme and quest for each Christian: *"The will of God, nothing less, nothing more, nothing else."*[11] May we as Christians strive to be like Him, giving up our will for His; submitting ourselves in full to Him for the purposes of His will daily. It is either following God, or following Satan by default. It is impossible to do both.

May He be pleased as we humbly bow, presenting ourselves as implements to be used however He sees fit. Above all things, may He be glorified by us; in our thoughts, in our words and in our deeds. Amen.

---

[1] Chuck Missler, *Alien Encounters* (Coeur d'Alene: Koinonia House 1997), 206
[2] Ibid
[3] Ibid, 207
[4] Ibid, 213
[5] Ibd, 240
[6] Stephen Quayle *Giants of Genesis 6* (Bozeman: End Time Thunder 2008)
[7] Paul Enns *The Moody Handbook of Theology*, (Chicago: Moody Press 1989), 62
[8] Ibid
[9] Arnold G. Fruchtenbaum, *The Footsteps of the Messiah* (San Antonio: Ariel Ministries), 635
[10] Ibid, 350
[11] Alan Redpath *The Life of Victory* (Great Britain: Christian Focus Publications 2000), 15

NOTES

Resources for Your Library:

BOOKS:

- Basis of the Premillennial Faith, The, by Charles C. Ryrie
- Biblical Hermeneutics, by Milton S. Terry
- Daniel, the Key to Prophetic Revelation by John F. Walvoord
- Dictionary of Premillennial Theology, Mal Couch, Editor
- Daniel, by H. A. Ironside
- Daniel: The Kingdom of the Lord, by Charles Lee Feinberg
- Daniel's Prophecy of the 70 Weeks, by Alva J. McClain
- Exploring the Future, by John Phillips
- Footsteps of the Messiah, by Arnold G. Fruchtenbaum
- For Zion's Sake: Christian Zionism and the Role of John Nelson Darby, by Paul Richard Wilkinson
- Future Israel (Why Christian Anti-Judaism Must Be Challenged), by E. Ray Clendenen, Ed.
- Giants Genesis 6, Stephen Quayle (www.stevequayle.com)
- God's Plan for Israel, Steven A. Kreloff
- Israel in the Plan of God, by David Baron
- Israelology, by Arnold G. Fruchtenbaum
- Moody Handbook of Theology, The by Paul Enns
- Most High God (Daniel), by Renald E. Showers
- Mountains of Israel, The, by Norma Archbold
- Pre-Wrath Rapture Answered, The, by Lee W. Brainard
- Prophecy 20/20 by Dr. Chuck Missler
- There Really Is a Difference! by Renald Showers
- Things to Come, by J. Dwight Pentecost
- What on Earth is God Doing? By Renald Showers

Order Other Books by Fred DeRuvo

www.createspace.com • www.amazon.com • www.rightly-dividing.com

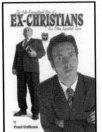

The Anti-Supernatural Bias of Ex-Christians (AVAILABLE)
Look into the testimonies of folks who refer to themselves as Ex-Christians. Are they, or are they kidding themselves? Fred goes back to the Bible to determine the truth of their words. Other topics deal with the Rapture, the Israelites as slaves in Egypt and more. 240 pages, $11.99, 7 x 10 format

When the Rightful Owner Returns (IN-PROGRESS)
Prophecy has become more of an interest to many Christians lately and with it, varying ideas related to the End Times. Is there any way to know for certain what the Bible actually teaches? Fred believes there is and it starts with a right understanding of the Bible. 235 pages, $10.99, 7 x 10 format

Christianity Practically Speaking (IN-PROGRESS)
As a Christian, do you ever feel like it's just not working, where the rubber meets the road? Is it your expectations, the Bible's, or a bit of both? Fred seeks to explain Christianity in practical terms that every Christian can appreciate. 235 pages, $10.99, 7 x 10 format

Unlocking Israel's Heart (IN-PROGRESS)
Romans chapters nine through eleven deal with Israel as it relates to the future. Paul seems clear enough that there is yet a future for Israel, yet not all would agree. Is there a way to be clear about what Paul says? Does the nation he loves have a future? 235 pages, $10.99, 7 x 10 format

Interpreting the Bible Literally (AVAILABLE)
unfortunately, too many Christians today are not aware that in order to study and interpret Scripture, certain tools (or methods) must be applied. It's like learning a foreign language, complete with idioms and other forms of figurative language. 235 pages, $10.99, 7 x 10 format

Made in the USA
Charleston, SC
19 January 2010